Praise for *The Circle Maker S*

I believe God desires to mark an entire gen power to see them burn for Him throughout whole lives.

If a generation is to fully step into all God has for them, then their foundation must be a life saturated in prayer. Mark Batterson has written a book that will ignite a passion for prayer in the foundational years of the teens and twenties. I believe this call to embrace the Lord's promises and declare His goodness and faithfulness will significantly impact readers for the rest of their lives.

There is no greater work than partnering with Heaven in prayer, and I am grateful Mark is releasing this message to a younger generation through *The Circle Maker Student Edition*. Whether you are a teenager, twenty-something, or a leader of young people, I highly recommend this book and ask the Lord to brand you for prayer.

Banning Liebscher
Director of Jesus Culture and author of *Jesus Culture: Living a Life that Transforms the World* and *The Journey of a World Changer: 40 Days to Ignite a Life that Transforms the World*

You've found it! Don't put this book down. What you're now holding in your hands is more than just another book on prayer. Mark Batterson's *Circle Maker Student Edition* is THE playbook for any teenager, youth pastor, or youth leader who wants to really leave their own mark on eternal history. As Mark shows you how to dream big, pray hard, and think long, God will unlock the destiny that you have been passionately looking for. Seriously ... Do yourself a favor and get this book. It's just that good!

Jeanne Mayo
President, Youth Leader's Coach International youth communicator, and leadership coach
Director of Youth and Young Adult Outreaches, Victory World Church, Norcross, Georgia

Praise for *The Circle Maker*

Mark Batterson's *The Circle Maker* will have you praying circles around any situation you are facing. You'll be inspired and motivated into a deeper level of prayer and faith.

> Craig Groeschel, senior pastor of LifeChurch.tv and author of *Weird: Because Normal Isn't Working*

Honi the circle maker is a longtime legendary figure, and Mark Batterson is well on his way. You will love the freshness of this approach to prayer.

> John Ortberg, pastor at Menlo Park Presbyterian Church in Menlo Park, California, and author of *The Me I Want to Be*

My bookshelves at home are littered with books I intended to read but never finished. Mark doesn't write those kinds of books. Mark writes books that demand a second and even third reading, because there's always something new to find. With *The Circle Maker*, Mark has done it again.

> Jon Acuff, *Wall Street Journal* bestselling author of *Quitter* and *Stuff Christians Like*

Mark Batterson encourages readers to take their prayer lives to a new level that will honor the mighty power of God. Like the man who made prayer circles for rain, we are to make bold prayers for things that seem impossible. Through the stories of modern-day prayer miracles, you will be inspired to draw prayer circles around your family, friends, and yourself. *The Circle Maker* teaches that God is for you and that the big dreams you claim in your prayers will be reflected in the way you live your life.

> Pastor Matthew Barnett, cofounder of the Dream Center

Mark Batterson is a master storyteller. His stories illustrate important biblical truths that convict me in my heart and make me hunger for a closer walk with God. *The Circle Maker* is such a story. I have changed the way I pray, longing for a more powerful and effective prayer life. I am now drawing circles.

> Ruth Graham, author of *Fear Not Tomorrow, God Is Already There*

The Circle Maker

STUDENT EDITION

Dream Big, Pray Hard, Think Long

Mark Batterson
with
Parker Batterson

ZONDERVAN.com/
AUTHORTRACKER
follow your favorite authors

ZONDERVAN

The Circle Maker Student Edition
Copyright © 2012 by Mark Batterson

This title is also available as a Zondervan ebook.
Visit www.zondervan.com/ebooks.

Requests for information should be addressed to:
Zondervan, Grand Rapids, Michigan 49530

ISBN 978-0-310-72513-8

Published in association with the literary agency of Fedd & Company, Inc., Post Office Box 341973, Austin, TX 78734.

Cover design: Cindy Davis
Interior illustration: iStockPhoto®
Interior design: Beth Shagene
Interior composition: Greg Johnson/Textbook Perfect

Printed in the United States of America

12 13 14 15 16 17 18 /DCI/ 22 21 20 19 18 17 16 15 14 13 12 11 10 9 8 7 6 5 4 3 2 1

*To an amazing father-in-law and grandfather, Bob Schmidgall.
The memory of you kneeling in prayer lives forever,
as do your prayers.*

Contents

Chapter 1

The Legend of the Circle Maker

Kids danced through the streets like it was the first rainfall they'd ever seen. And it was. Parents threw back their heads and caught every drop they could. When it hasn't rained in more than a year, every raindrop is a gift from God.

It would be forever remembered as *the day*. The day thunderclaps applauded the Almighty. The day puddle jumping became an act of praise. The day the legend of the circle maker was born.

If you know anything about the history of Israel, you know they hit some tough spots. But the first century BC was one of the worst. An entire generation was on the brink of death because of a drought. The Jewish prophets had been out of commission for hundreds of years. No one could remember a single miracle. And worst of all, God was nowhere to be heard. But there was one man who dared to pray anyway. His name was Honi.[1] And even if the people could no longer hear God, he believed that God could still hear them.

When it rains all the time, you don't give it a passing thought. During a drought, it's the only thought. And Honi was their only hope. Like the prophet Elijah before him, Honi was famous for his ability to pray for rain. It was on this day that Honi would earn his reputation.

With a six-foot staff in his hand, Honi began to turn like a math compass. His circular movement was rhythmical and methodical. Ninety degrees. One hundred eighty degrees. Two hundred seventy degrees. Three hundred sixty degrees. He never looked up as the crowd looked on. After what seemed like hours but had only been seconds, Honi stood inside the circle he had shaped with his staff.

Then he dropped to his knees and raised his hands to heaven. With the authority of the prophet Elijah, Honi called down rain:

"Lord of the universe, I swear before Your great name that I will not leave this circle until You have mercy upon Your children."

Everyone within earshot shivered. And though the words rang clear, the volume of his voice didn't nearly equal the authority of his tone. Not a hint of doubt. This prayer didn't come from his vocal chords — it flowed from the depth of his soul. His prayer was resolute yet humble, confident yet meek, expectant yet unassuming.

Then it happened.

As his prayer ascended to the heavens, raindrops descended to the earth. Now thousands of onlookers encircled Honi, and a gasp went through the crowd. All eyes looked to the sky as the first raindrops parachuted down, but Honi's head remained bowed. The people jumped for joy over every drop, but Honi wasn't satisfied with a sprinkle. Still kneeling within the circle, Honi lifted his voice over the sounds of celebration:

"Not for such rain have I prayed, but for rain that will fill cisterns, pits, and caverns."

The sprinkle turned into such a torrential downpour that the heavens roared. Eyewitnesses said every drop was the size of an egg! It rained so heavily and so steadily that the people fled to the Temple Mount to escape flash floods. Honi stayed and prayed in his fading circle. Once more he refined his bold request:

"Not for such rain have I prayed, but for rain of Your favor, blessing, and graciousness."

Then the perfect rain shower began to calmly cover the dead and thirsty ground, filling the air with a gentle, peaceful mist. Every raindrop was a sign of God's grace. And they didn't just soak the skin; they soaked the spirit and refreshed the faith of all who were there that day. It was difficult to believe the day before *the day*. The day after *the day*, it was impossible *not* to believe.

Eventually, the dirt turned into mud and back into dirt again.

After quenching their thirst, the crowd dispersed. And the rainmaker returned to his humble hovel on the outskirts of Jerusalem. Life did return to normal, but the legend of the circle maker had been born. And it introduced a new normal.

To the people, Honi was celebrated like a hometown hero. After all, he had saved their lives with his prayer. But some within the Sanhedrin complained about the circle maker. They said his prayer was too bold. They believed that drawing a circle and demanding rain dishonored God. Maybe it was those same members of the Sanhedrin who would criticize Jesus for healing a man's shriveled hand on the Sabbath a generation later. They actually threatened Honi with excommunication, but because they could not deny the miracle that had been performed, Honi was ultimately honored for his act of prayerful bravado.

The prayer that saved a generation was deemed one of the most significant prayers in the history of Israel. The circle he drew in the sand became a sacred symbol. And the legend of Honi the circle maker stands forever as a testament to the power of a single prayer to change the course of history.

Draw the Circle

1. What is your first reaction to Honi's story?
2. Why do you think God loves big dreams and bold prayers?
3. If one prayer has the power to change the course of history, why do you think we don't pray more?

Chapter 2

Circle Makers

The earth has circled the sun more than two thousand times since *the day* Honi drew his circle in the sand, but God is still looking for circle makers. It's as true now as it was then: *Bold prayers honor God* and *God honors bold prayers*. God isn't offended by your biggest dreams or boldest prayers. He is offended by anything less. If your prayers aren't impossible to you, they are insulting to God. Why? Because they don't require divine intervention. But ask God to part the Red Sea or make the sun stand still, and God is moved to omnipotent action.

There is nothing God loves more than keeping promises, answering prayers, performing miracles, and fulfilling dreams. That is *who* He is. That is *what* He does. And the bigger the circle we draw, the better, because God gets more glory. The greatest moments in life are the miraculous moments when human weakness and divine power intersect — and they intersect when we draw a circle around the impossible situations in our lives and invite God to intervene.

I can promise you one thing: God is ready and waiting. I have no idea what circumstances you find yourself in, but I can tell you that you are only one prayer away from a dream fulfilled, a promise kept, or a miracle performed.

It is absolutely critical at the very beginning that you come to terms with this simple yet life-changing truth: *God is for you.*[1] You need to know that God is on your side, God is in your corner! If you don't believe that, then you'll pray small, timid prayers. If you do believe it, then you'll pray big, audacious prayers. And one way or another, your small, timid prayers or big, audacious prayers will change the course of your life and turn you into two totally different people. Prayers are prophecies. They are the best forecast of your spiritual future. *Who you become* is determined by *how you pray*. Ultimately, the transcript of your prayers becomes the script of your life.

In the pages that follow, you'll encounter modern-day circle makers who will inspire you to dream big, pray hard, and think long. You'll discover how to claim God-given promises, pursue God-sized dreams, and seize God-ordained opportunities. You'll learn how to draw prayer circles around your family, your future, your problems, and your goals. But before I show you *how* to draw prayer circles, it's important to understand *why* it is so important. Drawing prayer circles isn't some magic trick to get what you want from God. God is not a genie in a bottle, and your wish is not His command. His command better be your wish. If it's not, you won't be drawing prayer circles. You'll just be walking in circles.

Drawing prayer circles starts with understanding what God wants, what God wills. And until His sovereign will becomes your holy wish, your prayer life will be unplugged from its power supply. Sure, you can apply some of the principles you learn in *The Circle Maker*, and they may help you get what you want, but getting what you want isn't the goal. The goal is getting what God wants for you, which is way better than what you could ever wish for anyway!

My First Circle

Over the years, I've drawn prayer circles around promises in Scripture and promises the Holy Spirit has conceived in my spirit. I've drawn prayer circles around impossible situations and impossible people. I've drawn prayer circles around everything from life goals to pieces of property. But before I get into those things, let me take you back to the first prayer circle I ever drew.

When I was a twenty-two-year-old graduate student, I tried to plant a church on the north shore of Chicago, but that plant never took root. Six months later, with a failed church plant on my résumé, my wife Lora and I moved from Chicago to Washington, DC. The opportunity to attempt another church plant presented itself, and my knee-jerk reaction was to say no way. But God gave me the courage to face my fears, swallow my pride, and try again.

There was nothing easy about our first year of church planting. Our total church income was $2,000 a month, and $1,600 of that went to rent the DC public school cafetorium where we held Sunday services. On a good Sunday, twenty-five people would show up. That's when I learned to close my eyes in worship because it was too depressing to open them. I had a lot of education at that point, but very little experience. I really had no idea how to lead (and that's challenging when you *are* the leader). I felt underqualified and overwhelmed, but that is when God has you right where He wants you. That is how you learn to live in raw dependence — and raw dependence is the raw material out of which God performs His greatest miracles.

One day, while dreaming about the church God wanted to establish on Capitol Hill, I was reading through the book of Joshua. A promise jumped off the page and into my spirit.

"I'm giving you every square inch of the land you set your foot on — just as I promised Moses."[2]

As I read that assurance given to Joshua, I felt that God wanted me to stake claim to the land He had called us to and pray a perimeter all the way around Capitol Hill. I had a Honi-like confidence that just as this promise had been transferred from Moses to Joshua, God would transfer the promise to me if I had enough faith to circle it.[3] So one hot and humid August morning, I drew what would be my first prayer circle. It still ranks as the longest prayer walk I've ever done and the biggest prayer circle I've ever drawn.

Starting at the front door of our row house on Capitol Hill, I walked east on F Street and turned south on 8th Street. I crossed East Capitol, the street that bisects the NE and SE quadrants of the city, and turned west on M Street SE. I then completed the circle, which was actually more of a square, by heading north on South Capitol Street. I paused to pray in front of the Capitol for a few minutes. Then I completed the 4.7-mile circle by taking a right turn at Union Station and heading home.

It's hard to describe what I felt when I finished drawing that circle. My feet were sore, but my spirit soared. I felt the same kind of holy confidence the Israelites must have felt when they crossed the Jordan River on dry ground and stepped foot in the Promised Land for the first time. I couldn't wait to see the way God would honor that prayer. That prayer circle had taken nearly three hours to complete because my prayer pace is slower than my normal pace, but God has been answering that three-hour prayer for the past fifteen years.

Since *the day* I drew that prayer circle around Capitol Hill, National Community Church (NCC) has grown into one church meeting in six movie theaters around the DC area. We're also on the verge of launching our first international location, a coffeehouse ministry in Berlin, Germany. And God has given us the privilege of influencing thousands of people over the last decade and a half. For what it's worth, nearly 70 percent of the people in our church are single twenty-somethings.

All Bets Are Off

As I look back, I'm grateful for the miracles God has done. I'm also keenly aware of the fact that every miracle has a genealogy. If you trace those miracles all the way back to their origin, you'll find a prayer circle. Miracles are the by-product of prayers that were prayed *by you* or *for you*. And that should be all the motivation you need to pray.

God has determined that certain expressions of His power will only be exercised in response to prayer. Simply put, God won't do it unless you pray for it. We have not because we ask not, or maybe I should say, we have not because we circle not. The greatest tragedy in life is the prayers that go unanswered because they go unasked.

Now here's the good news: If you do pray, all bets are off. You aren't called to live in the shadow of doubt. Instead, you can live with a holy anticipation because you never know how or when or where God is going to answer your prayers. But I promise you this: He will answer. He may not answer *when* or *how* you want. But it will be the right answer at the right time. And His answers are not limited by your requests. We pray out of our ignorance, but God answers out of His omniscience. We pray out of our limited human understanding, but God answers out of His unlimited knowledge. God has the ability to answer the prayers we should have prayed but lacked the knowledge or ability to even ask.

During my prayer walk around Capitol Hill, I drew circles around things I didn't even know how to ask for. Without even knowing it, I drew prayer circles around people who would one day come to faith in Jesus Christ at our coffeehouse on Capitol Hill (which wasn't even an idea at that point). Without even knowing it, I walked right by a piece of property at 8th Street and Virginia Avenue SE that we would purchase thirteen years later as a result of a $3 million gift that wasn't even a prayer yet. Without even knowing it, I walked right under a theater marquee on Barracks Row, the main street of Capitol Hill, that we would renovate and reopen as our seventh location fifteen years later. It's the oldest operational theater in the nation's capital, and we get to determine what is played on the screen!

Those answers are a testament to the power of God and a reminder that if you draw prayer circles, God will answer those prayers somehow, someway, sometime. God has been answering that one prayer for fifteen years, and He'll keep answering it forever. Just like Honi, your prayers have the potential to change the course of history.

It's time to start circling.

Draw the Circle

1. Why do you think some people pray like God is *against them* instead of believing that God is *for them*? Have you ever felt that way?

2. Drawing circles begins with understanding what God wants and what God wills. Have you ever prayed for something that you later discovered wasn't really God's will? What was that like?

3. What does this statement mean to you, and why is it true?: "If your prayers aren't impossible to you, they are insulting to God."

Chapter 3

The Jericho Miracle

Every book has a backstory. There is a moment when an idea is conceived in the imagination of an author and this idea is destined to become a book. And because I believe the backstory will help you appreciate the story, let me share the genesis of *The Circle Maker*.

I developed an appetite for reading during my senior year of college. I spent all my spare cash and spare time on books. Since then, I've read thousands of books on topics ranging from neurology to biography to astronomy, and a few fiction titles too. My bookshelves are so filled with books that I have them stacked on top of my shelves as high as I can reach. I even have stacks on my floor in precarious piles that look like the Leaning Tower of Pisa. I ran out of shelf space a few years ago, which means that not every book "makes the shelf." I do have one shelf, however, that contains only my favorites, a few dozen of them. One of them is titled *The Book of Legends*.

The Book of Legends is a collection of stories from the Talmud and Midrash. In other words, it contains the teachings of Jewish rabbis passed down from generation to generation. Because it contains more than a millennium's worth of wisdom, reading *The Book of Legends* feels like an archaeological dig. I had dug down 202 pages when I stumbled across a story that may as well have been a buried treasure. It was the legend of Honi the circle maker. And it forever changed the way I pray.

I've always believed in the power of prayer. It's the spiritual inheritance I received from my grandparents. I had a grandfather who would kneel by his bedside at night, take off his hearing aid, and pray for his family. He couldn't hear himself without his hearing aid on, but everyone else in the house could. Few things leave as lasting an impression as hearing someone genuinely intercede for you. And even though he died when I was six, his prayers did not. Our prayers never die. There have been moments in my life when the Spirit of God has whispered to my spirit, *Mark, the prayers of your grandfather are being answered in your life right now.* That's when I realized that my grandfather had been praying circles around me before I was even born.

The legend of Honi the circle maker was like a revelation of the power of prayer. It gave me a new vocabulary, a new imagery, a new methodology. It not only inspired me to pray bold prayers but also helped me pray with more length and intensity. I started circling everyone and everything in prayer. I drew particular inspiration from the march around Jericho, when God delivered on a four-hundred-year-old promise by providing the first victory in the Promised Land. While the story doesn't explicitly mention the people taking up positions of prayer, I have no doubt that the Israelites were praying as they circled the city. Isn't that what you instinctively do when you face a challenge that is way beyond your ability? The Israelites circling Jericho for seven days is the image of what drawing prayer circles looks like. It's also the backdrop for this book.

Jericho March

The first glimpse of Jericho was both awe-inspiring and frightening. While wandering in the wilderness for forty years, the Israelites had never seen anything like the skyline of Jericho. The closer they got, the smaller they felt. They finally understood why the generation before them felt so miniscule and failed to enter the Promised Land because of fear.[1]

A six-foot-wide lower wall and fifty-foot-high upper wall encircled the ancient metropolis. The mud-brick walls were so thick and tall that the twelve-acre city appeared to be an impenetrable fortress. It seemed like God had promised something impossible, and His battle plan made zero sense: *Your entire army is to march around the city once a day for six days. On the seventh day you are to march around the city seven times.*[2]

Every soldier in the army had to have wondered why. Why not use a battering ram? Why not scale the walls? Why not cut off the water supply or shoot flaming arrows over the walls? Instead, God told the Israelite army to silently circle the city. And He promised that after they circled thirteen times over those seven days, the walls would crumble.

The first time around, the soldiers must have felt kind of dumb. But with each circle, their stride grew a little longer. With each circle, a holy confidence was building pressure inside their souls. By the seventh day, their faith was ready to pop. They got up before dawn and started circling at six o'clock in the morning. Let's pull out some algebra here: at three miles per hour, each mile-and-a-half march around the city took a half hour. (See? Algebra does apply to real life.) By nine o'clock, they began their final lap. In keeping with God's command, they hadn't said a word in six days. They just silently circled the promise. Then the priests sounded their horns, and a simultaneous shout followed. Six hundred thousand Israelites sent up a roar and, as the song goes, the walls came tumbling down.

After seven days of circling Jericho, God delivered on a four-hundred-year-old promise. He proved, once again, that His promises don't have expiration dates. And Jericho stands, and falls, as evidence to this simple truth: If you keep circling the promise, God will ultimately deliver on it.

What Is Your Jericho?

This miracle is a microcosm.

Simply put, it both reveals the way God performed this particular miracle and also establishes a pattern to follow. It challenges us to confidently circle the promises God has given to us. It forces us to ask: What is your Jericho?

For the Israelites, Jericho symbolized the fulfillment of a dream that began with Abraham. It was the first step in claiming the Promised Land. It was the miracle they had been hoping for and waiting for their entire lives.

What is your Jericho?

What promise are you praying around? What miracle are you marching around? What dream does your life revolve around?

Drawing prayer circles starts with identifying your Jericho. You've got to define the promises God wants you to stake claim to, the miracles God wants you to believe for, and the dreams God wants you to pursue. Then you need to keep circling until God gives you what He wants and He wills. That's the goal. Now here's the problem: Most of us don't get what we want simply because we don't know what we want. We've never circled any of God's promises. We've never written down a list of life goals. We've never defined success for ourselves. Instead of drawing circles, we draw blanks.

Circling Jericho

More than a thousand years after the Jericho miracle, another miracle happened in the exact same place. Jesus is on His way out of Jericho when two blind men hail Him like he's a taxi-driver: "Lord, Son of David, have mercy on us!" The disciples see it as a human interruption. Jesus sees it as a divine appointment. So He stops and responds with a pointed question: "What do you want me to do for you?"[3]

Seriously? Is that question even necessary? Isn't it obvious what they want? They're blind. Yet Jesus forced them to define exactly what they wanted from Him. He made them spell it out, but it wasn't because Jesus didn't know what they wanted (believe me, He knew); He wanted to make sure *they knew* what they wanted. And that is where drawing prayer circles begins: knowing what to circle.

What if Jesus were to ask you this very same question: *What do you want me to do for you?* Would you be able to spell out the promises, miracles, and dreams God has put in your heart? I'm afraid many of us would be dumbfounded. Sure there are things we could ask Him for, like an iPhone, but really, what's *worth* asking Jesus for? We have no idea what we want God to do for us. If we can't answer this question, then we're as blind spiritually as these blind men were physically.

So while God is for us, most of us have no idea what we want God to do for us. And that's why our prayers aren't just boring to us; they are uninspiring to God. When there's no real thought behind your prayers, it's as lame for Him to listen as it is for you to pray it. If faith is being sure of what we hope for, then being unsure of what we hope for is the exact opposite of faith, isn't it? Well-developed faith results in well-defined prayers, and well-defined prayers result in a well-lived life.

If you read this book without answering this question, you will have missed the point. Like the two blind men outside Jericho, you need an encounter with the Son of God. You need an answer to the question He is still asking: What do you want me to do for you?

Obviously, the answer to this question changes over time. We need different miracles during different seasons of life. We pursue different dreams during different stages of life. We claim different promises in different situations. It's a moving target, but you have to start somewhere. Why not here and now? No time better than the present.

Don't just read the Bible. Start circling the promises with a pen and with prayer. Don't just make a wish. Write down a list of God-glorifying life goals. Don't just pray. Keep a prayer journal. God loves when you make an effort.

Spell It Out

Jericho is spelled many different ways. If your grandfather has cancer, it's spelled *healing*. If your best friend is far from God, it's spelled *salvation*. If your family is falling apart and shattered, it's spelled *reconciliation*. If you have a dream beyond your finances, it's spelled *provision*. If you feel broken and hurting, it's spelled *hope*. But whatever it is, you have to spell it out. Sometimes Jericho is spelled without letters. It's a zip code you're called to or a dollar figure that you need to give. And sometimes Jericho has the same spelling as someone's name. For me, Jericho has three different spellings: Parker, Summer, and Josiah.

When my friend Wayne and his wife, Diane, were expecting their first child, they started praying for their baby. They believed prayer was their primary parental responsibility, so why wait till their baby was born? Every evening, Wayne would lay hands on Diane's stomach and pray the promises in Scripture that they had circled for their baby. During the first part of their pregnancy, they came across a book that said it was never too early to start praying for their baby's future spouse. At first it seemed odd praying for a spouse before they even knew the gender of their baby, but they prayed for their baby and their baby's spouse day after day until their due date.

Wayne and Diane decided to wait until birth to discover their baby's gender, but they prayed that God would reveal what the baby's name should be. In October 1983, the Lord gave them a girl's name. It was spelled Jessica. Then in December, the Lord gave them a boy's name, and they started praying for Timothy. They weren't sure why God had given them two different names, but they prayed circles around both Jessica and Timothy until Diane gave birth.

On May 5, 1984, God answered their prayers, and the answer was spelled Timothy. Wayne and Diane continued to circle their son in prayer, but they also kept praying for the girl that he would one day marry. Twenty-two years and two weeks of accumulated prayers culminated on May 19, 2006 — the day Timothy's bride walked down the aisle. Her name? You guessed it: Jessica.

Here's the rest of the story.

Their future daughter-in-law was born on October 19, 1983, the same month that God happened to give them the name Jessica. A thousand miles away, Wayne and Diane were praying for her by name. They thought Jessica would be their daughter, not their daughter-in-law, but God always has a surprise up His sovereign sleeve. For Wayne and Diane, Jericho has two spellings — Timothy and Jessica — but the same last name.

In case you're wondering, Timothy was allowed to date girls who weren't named Jessica! Wayne and Diane didn't even tell Timothy that God had given them the name of his future spouse before he was born until after he was engaged.

I have the joy of serving as Timothy and Jessica's pastor. So while Timothy and Jessica are the primary recipients of their parents' prayers, I get something out of it too. Besides a great story, they've been a huge blessing to NCC as small group leaders. And like any good story about blessing, it traces back to a prayer circle.

Vague Prayers

A few years ago, I read one sentence that dramatically changed the way I pray. The author/pastor of one of the largest churches in Seoul, Korea, wrote, "God does not answer vague prayers." When I read that statement, I was rocked by how vague my prayers were. Some of them were so vague that there was literally no way of knowing whether God had answered them or not.

It was during this spiritual season, when God was challenging me to spell out my prayers with greater specificity, that I embarked on a ten-day Pentecost fast. Try this sometime! Just like the 120 believers who prayed in an upper room for ten days, I prayed for ten days leading up to the day of Pentecost. I also felt led to pass on the great American pastime — eating. My rationale was pretty simple: If we do what they did in the Bible, we might experience the miracles they experienced in the Bible. You can't manufacture a miracle like Pentecost, but if you pray for ten days, a miracle like Pentecost might just happen.

During that ten-day Pentecost no-food fast, I was teaching a series at our church on miracles, and we had just experienced one. We miraculously purchased a piece of Promised Land that we had circled in prayer for more than five years. We took stones that had been laid in the foundation and gave one to everyone as tangible tokens of the miracle God had performed for NCC. Drawing on that corporate faith, we challenged people to personalize the question Jesus posed to the two blind men outside of Jericho: *What do you want me to do for you?* Then we wrote down our holy desires on those stones.[4] I spelled out seven miracles and started circling them in prayer.

In the spirit of full disclosure, not all seven of the miracles I asked for have happened. In fact, one of them even seemed to backfire. I asked God to give us the movie theaters at Union Station where our church met for more than a decade, but instead of giving us the theaters, He took them away. The theaters were unexpectedly closed down, and we were given less than one week's notice to scram. It was pretty depressing and disorienting at the time, but I have to admit that this apparent "anti-miracle" was the start of some bigger and better miracles that have happened in its wake. What seemed like the wrong answer turned out to be the best answer. So not every prayer will be answered exactly the way we word it, but I'm convinced of this: The miracles that have happened would not have happened if I hadn't drawn a circle around them in the first place.

The more faith you have, the more specific your prayers will be. And the more specific your prayers are, the more glory God will get. Honi prayed for a specific type of rain, and so nuanced prayers give God an opportunity to reveal more shades of His power. If our prayers aren't specific, however, God gets robbed of the glory that He deserves because we second-guess whether or not He actually answered them. We never know if the answers were the result of specific prayer or general coincidences that would have happened anyway.

That stone with seven miracles written on it sits on a shelf in my office. Occasionally I'll pick it up and hold it in my hand while I pray. There isn't anything magical about it, but it acts as prayer insurance. It insures that I don't forget what I'm praying for. It also insures I pay up and give God all the credit when the miracles do happen.

The Ladder of Success

It's easy to get so busy climbing the ladder of success — getting good grades so we can go to a good school so we can get a good job and earn good money — that we fail to realize that the ladder is not leaning against the wall of Jericho. We get distracted from our God-ordained goals. Our everyday responsibilities overwhelm our eternal priorities. It's sad to see people sell out their God-given dream for the American dream. So instead of circling Jericho, we end up wandering in the wilderness for forty years.

If you're like me, you always have somewhere to go or something to do. But a few years ago, I enjoyed a rare day without any agenda. I had just dropped off my family at the LAX airport after an excellent spring break in southern California. I stayed behind to speak at a leadership conference, but I had one day in between with nowhere to go and nothing to do, so I found a Starbucks along the Third Street Promenade in Santa Monica and spent the day circling Jericho.

That margin, along with a little California sunshine, made room for an epiphany. As I sipped my White Chocolate Mocha, it dawned on me that I had never really defined success for myself. I had written a couple books and started traveling on the speaking circuit, but neither of those goals was as fulfilling as I thought they would be. I often felt excitement mixed with a profound sadness as I scrambled through airport security on my way to whatever speaking destination was next. My life reminded me of the joke I would sometimes tell about the airline pilot who came over the intercom and said, "I have good news and bad news. The bad news is we're lost; the good news is we're making great time." That's what my life felt like, but it wasn't a joke.

I've never met anyone who was going through their teen years thinking they didn't want to be successful, but very few teenagers and young adults have actually spelled out success for themselves. We inherit our family expectations or believe our close friend's popular opinion. We allow all of our social platforms to give our life definition. But if you don't spell it out for yourself, you have no way of knowing if you've achieved it. You might achieve your goals only to realize that they should not have been your goals in the first place. You circle the wrong city. You climb the wrong ladder.

Variant Spellings

As window-shoppers strolled up and down the promenade, I scribbled a personal definition of success on a napkin. That napkin may as well have been a stone tablet inscribed by the finger of God on Mount Sinai. God redefined success and spelled it out for me on that napkin. Like definitions in the dictionary that capture different dimensions of a word, I jotted down three variant spellings.

The first definition may sound generic, but it's specific to any and every situation:

1. *Do the best you can with what you have where you are.* Success isn't circumstantial. We usually focus on what we're doing or where we're going, but God's primary concern is *who we're becoming* in the process. We talk about "doing" the will of God as if it's an action, but the will of God has much more to do with "being" than "doing." It's

not about being in the right place at the right time (as some bad situations are impossible to avoid); it's about being the right person, even if you find yourself in the wrong circumstances. Success has nothing to do with how gifted or how resourced you are. Success is the kind of person you become. Success is making the most of every gift you've been given and every situation you find yourself in.

The second definition I wrote down captures my calling. Whether I'm writing or speaking or spending time with my family, this is the driving passion of my life:

2. *Help people maximize their God-given potential.* Potential is God's gift to us; what we do with it is our gift back to God. Helping people maximize their God-given potential is why God put me on this planet. That is what gets me up early and keeps me up late. Nothing is more exhilarating to me than seeing people grow into their God-given giftedness.

The third definition is my most genuine desire:

3. *My desire is that the people who know me the best respect me the most.* Success is not measured by how many people I pastor or how many books I sell, or how many people follow me on Facebook or Twitter; success is living life with such authentic integrity that those who know me best actually respect me most. I couldn't care less about fame or fortune. I want to be famous in my family! That is the greatest fortune.

If you don't have a personal definition of success, chances are you will "succeed" at the wrong thing. You'll get to the point of no return and realize that you spelled success wrong. And in life, not just English class, spelling does indeed count.

You need to circle the goals God wants you to go after, the promises God wants you to claim, and the dreams God wants you to pursue. And once you spell Jericho, you need to circle it in prayer. Then keep circling until the walls come tumbling down.

Get Outside the Walls

Circling Jericho gave the Israelites a 360-degree perspective of the walled promise. It helped them wrap their spirits around the mudbrick miracle. It gave definition to the fifty-foot-high dream. That is precisely what prayer does. It helps you get outside the problem. It helps you circle the miracle. It helps you see all the way around the situation.

Don't read this book without finding a time and finding a place to circle Jericho. Take a prayer retreat. Take a prayer journal. Get alone with God, or if you're wired for processing things through being with people over personal, private processing, then take some friends with you. They can form a prayer circle around you.

If you can, go someplace that inspires you. Combine what you love with the God that you love. Love nature? Take a hike through the woods or up a mountain. A change in scenery often translates into a change of perspective. A change in routine often results in revelation. Simple formula: change of pace + change of place = change of perspective.

I've always subscribed to Arthur McKinsey's method of problem solving: think of it as *prayer solving.*

> If you think of a problem as being like a medieval walled city, then a lot of people will attack it head-on, like a battering ram. They will storm the gates and try to smash through the defenses with sheer intellectual power and brilliance. I just camp outside the city. I wait. And I think. Until one day—maybe after I've turned to a completely different problem—the drawbridge comes down and the defenders say, "We surrender." The answer to the problem comes all at once.[5]

The Israelites didn't conquer Jericho because of a brilliant military strategy or brute force. They learned how to let the Lord fight their battles for them. Drawing prayer circles is far more powerful than any battering ram. Why try to do for yourself what only God can do for you? Prayer circles don't just knock down doors; they level fifty-foot walls.

When I retrace the miracles in my own life, I'm amazed at how many of them happened outside the city walls. They didn't happen during a planning meeting; they happened during a prayer meeting. It wasn't problem solving that won the day; it was prayer solving. I got outside the city walls and marched around the promise, around the problem, around the situation. And when you do that, it won't just be the drawbridge that drops; the wall will fall.

Draw the Circle

1. What are some blessings or miracles in your life that you believe are the result of someone else's prayers for you?

2. What is your Jericho? What promises has God given you that you are circling or staking claim to? What dreams does God want you to pursue?

3. Take a moment to spell out your personal definition of success. Be specific! Now, circle it in prayer.

Chapter 4

Praying Through

Before there was a Mother Teresa there was a Mother Dabney. In 1925, Elizabeth J. Dabney and her husband went to work for a mission in the City of Brotherly Love, but there wasn't much love in her neighborhood. Let's be straight: it was pretty much a hellhole. Her husband was called to preach. She was called to prayer, but she didn't just pray; she *prayed through.*

One afternoon when she was thinking about a bad situation in their North Philly neighborhood, she asked God if He would give them a spiritual victory if she made a deal with Him to pray. He promised that He would, and she felt the Lord prompting her to meet Him the next morning at the Schuylkill River at 7:30 a.m. sharp. Mother Dabney was so nervous about missing her prayer appointment that she stayed up all night crocheting.

The next morning she went down to the river outside the city walls, and the Lord said, "This is the place." The presence of God eclipsed her and she drew a circle in the sand:

Lord, if You will bless my husband in the place You sent him to establish Your name, if You will break the bonds and destroy the middle wall of partition, if You will give him a church and congregation — a credit to Your people and all Christendom — I will walk with You for three years in prayer, both day and night. I will meet You every morning at 9:00 a.m. sharp; You will never have to wait for me; I will be there to greet You. I will stay there all day; I will devote all of my time to You.

Furthermore, if You will listen to the voice of my supplication and break through in that wicked neighborhood and bless my husband, I will fast seventy-two hours each week for two years. While I am going through the fast, I will not go home to sleep in my bed. I will stay in church, and if I get sleepy, I'll rest on newspapers and carpet.[1]

As soon as she made that prayer covenant, it was like a cloud had burst. God's splendor fell from heaven like the raindrops that drenched Honi. Every morning at 9:00 a.m., Mother Dabney greeted the Lord with a hearty, "Good morning, Jesus." She wore the skin off her numb knees, but God extended His powerful right arm. She fasted seventy-two hours each week, and the Holy Spirit was her strength.

Soon their mission was too small to accommodate the people. Her husband asked her to pray for another meeting place nearby. She prayed, and a man who had been in business for twenty-five years closed up shop so they could rent the building. Mother Dabney would not be denied. She was a circle maker, and circle makers have a trademark stubborn streak.

Mother Dabney was more comfortable in the presence of God than the presence of people. As it was with Honi, some even criticized the way she prayed. Well-meaning friends begged her to take a break or take a bite, but she held on to the promise she made to the Lord. And the more she prayed through, the more God came through.

Mother Dabney's prayer legacy would be a long-forgotten footnote if it weren't for one headline. The *Pentecostal Evangel* published her testimony under the title "What It Means to Pray Through." That one article sparked a prayer movement all around the world. Mother Dabney received more than three million letters from people who wanted to learn how to pray through.

Counterfactual Theory

Circle makers tend to be history makers as well.

In the grand scheme of God's story, there is a footnote behind every headline. The footnote is prayer. And if you focus on the footnotes, God will write the headlines. It's your prayers that change the eternal plotline. Just like Honi's prayer that saved a generation, your prayers can change the course of history (or, as I like to spell it, "His-story").

I love history, and in particular, a branch of history called counterfactual theory. Counterfactual theorists ask the *what if* questions. What if the American Revolution had failed? Or what if Hitler had been victorious in World War II? How would history have unfolded differently? And what are the key footnotes that would have or could have changed the headlines of history?

Reading biblical history like a counterfactual theorist is worth trying. And the Jericho miracle is a great example. What if the Israelites had stopped circling on the sixth day? The answer is obvious. They would have forfeited the miracle right before it happened. If they had stopped circling after twelve round trips, they would have done a lot of walking for nothing. Like the generation before them, they would have missed out on the promise. And the same is true for us.

I've already stated our first problem: most of us don't get what we want because we don't know what we want. Here's our secondary problem: *Most of us don't get what we want because we quit circling.*

We give up too easily. We give up too quickly. We quit praying right before the miracle happens.

Praying For Versus Praying Through

We desperately need to rediscover the difference between *praying for* and *praying through*. There are certainly circumstances where praying for something will get the job done. Trust me, I believe in short prayers before meals because, quite frankly, I believe in eating food while it's still hot. But there are also situations where you need to lock yourself in and refuse to disconnect from God until He answers. Like Honi, you refuse to move from the circle until God moves. Simply put: intercede until God intervenes.

Praying through is all about consistency. It's circling Jericho so many times it makes you dizzy. Like the story Jesus told about the persistent widow who drove the judge crazy with her relentless requests, praying through means not taking no for an answer.[2] Circle makers know that it's always too soon to quit praying because you never know when the wall is about to fall. You are always only one prayer away from a miracle. That's what makes prayer so unpredictable — and exciting.

Praying through is all about intensity. Ever heard someone make completely guttural noises while they pray, or bawling with their hands tightly clenched? Drawing prayer circles involves more than words; it's literally about sweat and tears. That is what gets our heavenly Father's attention.

When was the last time you found yourself flat on your face in prayer? When was the last time you got sore knees kneeling before the Lord? When was the last time you pulled an all-nighter in prayer?

There will always be higher heights and deeper depths in prayer, and God wants to take you there. He wants to take you places you have never been before. There are new dialects. There are new dimensions. But if you want God to do something new in your life, you can't do the same old thing. You've got to do something different. It will involve more sacrifice, but you'll get to a place where you're so close to God that you will realize that you sacrificed very little in comparison to what you receive.

The Last Piece of Property on Capitol Hill

Have you ever faced something you felt you were meant to do, and nothing seemed to go the way you'd imagined? After the seeming anti-miracle of the movie theaters at Union Station closing, our church began checking out property on Capitol Hill to build an urban campus that would include a coffeehouse, performance theater, and centralized offices for our multisite staff. With a going price of $14 million an acre and very few properties on the market, I wondered if we were looking for something that didn't exist. After an exhaustive search, we found only one piece of property that met our specifications, so we dubbed it "the last piece of property on Capitol Hill." And the location was absolutely perfect — right where Capitol Hill and the Navy Yard meet. And the front of the property faced the expressway that is the main artery running through the heart of DC, giving it great visibility and accessibility.

The first time I set foot on that property at the corner of 8th Street and Virginia Avenue SE, it felt like standing on Promised Land. For several weeks, I silently circled that city block in prayer like the soldiers who marched around Jericho. Then, just before making an official offer, our leadership team met our realtor at the property for one last look. We were filled with excitement as we dreamed about the possibilities, but our dreams were just about destroyed less than twenty minutes later when our realtor called to inform me that a real estate developer had put a contract on the property *as we had been standing on it.*

I was deeply disappointed because I had already envisioned our new campus on that site. I was deeply confused because I felt like it was where God wanted us. But we should praise God for disappointment because it drives us to our knees. If we respond to it the right way, disappointment can actually restore our prayer rhythm and resurrect our dreams.

Later on that evening, our family knelt in prayer. One of our kids prayed a simple prayer: "God, I pray that this property would be used for Your glory." Right then and there, my faith found a heartbeat. I sensed in my spirit that God was going to give us that property. I believed it would belong to us because I knew that it belonged to God. So for three months we circled that property in prayer. I marched around that block like the Israelites marched around Jericho. I knelt on the property. I laid hands on the old glass company that had occupied the lot since 1963. I pulled out all the stops, and I even took off shoes like Joshua did before the battle of Jericho because I believed it was holy ground.

Out of Luck

At the end of the sixty-day feasibility period, the real estate developer who held the primary contract on the property asked for ten additional days to secure financing. That seemed like our window of opportunity so we offered a nonrefundable deposit (that means we basically gave them free money), and the owner told us he would give us the contract. We thought God had answered our prayers, but we weren't done circling. Twenty-four hours later, the owner changed his mind, and we lost the contract a second time!

Finally, at the end of the ten-day extension, I anxiously awaited word from our realtor. I was hoping that the third time would be a charm — not three strikes and you're out. I got the text on a Friday night while our family was at the theater watching *The Karate Kid*. I was enjoying the remake of the original movie, but his text message ruined it for me. He double-thumbed the bad news: "We're out of luck." Then this Spirit-inspired thought fired across my synapses: We may be out of luck, but we're not out of prayer.

Despite losing the contract a third time, I somehow still believed that God was going to defy the odds and give us our Promised Land. Sometimes faith seems like a denial of reality, but that's because we're holding on to a reality that is more real than the reality we can perceive with our five senses. We didn't have a physical contract on that property, but we had a spiritual contract on it via prayer. And a spiritual contract is more binding than a written contract.

A few days after our third strike, I flew to Peru to hike the Inca Trail to Machu Picchu with my son, Parker. For four days we were out of communication with civilization. When we arrived at Aguas Calientes, a small town at the foot of the Andes Mountain range, I called Lora from a public telephone booth. I'm sure onlookers wondered why a large American was jumping up and down inside a small telephone booth, but I was overwhelmed by the news Lora shared with me: *We got the contract!* I couldn't believe it, but I could believe it. We prayed through, and God came through.

I couldn't help but chuckle at the circumstances. It's almost like God said, *Let's get Mark out of the way so we can get this deal done.* In retrospect, I think God wanted me out of the country and out of communication so there was no mistaking it for what it was: a Jericho miracle.

Praise Through

Now let me backtrack. Let me reverse-engineer this miracle.

During the feasibility period, when the real estate developer had the primary contract on the property, I was rereading the story of the

Jericho miracle, and I noticed something I had never seen before. During devotions one day, a single phrase jumped off the page and into my spirit:

> Now the gates of Jericho were securely barred because of the Israelites. No one went out and no one came in. Then the LORD said to Joshua, "See, I have delivered Jericho into your hands."[3]

Did you catch the verb tense? God speaks in the *past tense*, not the *future tense*. He doesn't say, "I will deliver." God says, "I have delivered." The significance is this: The battle was won before the battle even began. God had already given them the city. All they had to do was circle it.

As I read this story, I felt as though the Spirit of God said to my spirit, "Stop praying for it and start praising me for it." True faith doesn't just celebrate after the miracle has already happened; true faith celebrates before the miracle happens, as if the miracle has already happened, because you know that you know that God is going to deliver on His promise.

This is going to sound a little contradictory, but sometimes you need to quit praying. After you pray through, you need to *praise through*. Yup, even after praying hard there is more work to do. You have to praise as hard as you can. Prayer and praise are both expressions of faith, but praise is a higher dimension of faith. Prayer is asking God to do something, future tense; praise is believing that God has already done it, past tense.

Before you write this off as some "name it, claim it" scheme, let me remind you that God cannot be bribed or blackmailed. Remember that. God doesn't do miracles to satisfy our selfish whims. God does miracles for one reason and one reason alone: to spell His glory. We just so happen to be the beneficiaries.

Keep Circling Jericho

Not long after making this devotional discovery, I shared this past-tense principle with our church. We literally stopped praying that God would give us the property. We started praising Him for it because we felt like God had promised it.

If God has put a promise in your heart, praise Him for it. You need to celebrate as if it has already happened. Stop asking because God has already answered. And for the record, even if God doesn't answer the way you want, you still need to praise through. That's when it's most difficult to praise God, but that is also when our praise is most pure and most pleasing to God.

Right after God gave me this revelation, I went over to the property we were praying for, got down on my knees, and started praising God for the promise He had put in my heart. We lost that contract three separate times, but we kept praising God. The deal died three times, but resurrection is the central part of the Christian faith. It isn't something we just celebrate on Easter. Resurrection is something we celebrate every day in every way! Prayer has the power to resurrect dead dreams and give them new life — better yet, eternal life.

I'm not sure what promise God has put in your heart. I don't know what dream you're holding on to or what miracle you're holding out for, but I offer this encouragement: Keep circling Jericho.

And don't just pray through; praise through.

Draw the Circle

1. What does it mean to "pray through"? Have you ever done it?

2. We often quit praying too easily or too quickly. Have you ever stopped circled something in prayer too soon?

3. How would you feel if others expressed their love to you only when you gave them what they desired? So often, we give God praise only after our prayer is answered. What areas might you be praying through that God is now telling you to praise through for the outcome?

Part 1

The First Circle — Dream Big

Until the day he died, Honi the circle maker was mesmerized by one phrase in one verse of Scripture — Psalm 126:1. "When the LORD restored the fortunes of Zion, we were like those who dreamed." That phrase, "we were like those who dreamed," ended up provoking a question that Honi grappled with his entire life:

Is it possible for a man to dream continuously for seventy years?[1]

Neuroimaging (bear with me here) is basically a medical scan of the brain and nervous system. It's shown that as we age, we think a little differently. We move from more of an imaginative right brain as teenagers to a more logical left brain as adults. (Good to know there's a reason why your parents sometimes act the way they do. Too often, I'm sure.) Problem is, this neurological tendency presents a pretty serious spiritual danger. At some point, most of us stop living out of imagination and start living out of memory. Instead of creating the future, we start repeating the past. Instead of living by faith, we live by logic. Instead of going after our dreams, we stop circling Jericho.

But it doesn't have to be that way.

As we age, either creativity overtakes memory or memory overtakes creativity. Imagination is the road less traveled, but I think it's the pathway of prayer. Prayer and imagination are directly proportional: the more you pray the bigger your imagination becomes because the Holy Spirit supersizes it with God-sized dreams. A good test of spiritual maturity is whether your dreams are getting bigger or smaller. The older you get, the more faith you should have, because you've experienced more of God's faithfulness. And it's God's faithfulness that should increase our faith and expand our vision.

Is it possible for a man to dream continuously for seventy years?

In classic Honi fashion, he answered his question with his own life. He never stopped dreaming because he never stopped praying. And how could he, after God answered his just-about-impossible prayer for rain? Once you've experienced a miracle like that, you believe God can do way bigger and better miracles.

If you keep praying, you'll keep dreaming, and better yet, if you keep dreaming, you'll keep praying. Dreaming really is a form of praying, and praying is a form of dreaming. The more you pray the bigger your dreams will become. And the bigger your dreams become, the more you have to pray.

The day we stop dreaming is the day we start dying. When vision is sacrificed on the altar of logic, God is robbed of the glory that rightfully belongs to Him. In fact, the death of a dream is often a subtle form of idolatry. We lose faith in the God who gave us the big dream and settle for a small dream that we can accomplish without His help. We go after dreams that don't require divine intervention. Lame. And the God who is able to do immeasurably more than all our right brain can imagine is undermined by a god — a god who doesn't even get a capital G — who fits within the logical boundaries of our left brain.

Nothing honors God more than a big dream that is way beyond our ability to accomplish. Why? Because there's no way we can take credit for it. And nothing is better for our spiritual development than a big dream because it keeps us on our knees in raw dependence on God. Drawing prayer circles around our dreams isn't just a mechanism for accomplishing great things for God; it's a mechanism God uses to accomplish great things in us.

Is it possible for a man to dream continuously for seventy years?

If you keep drawing prayer circles, the answer is yes.

Keep dreaming until the day you die. Let creativity overtake memory. May you die young at a ripe old age!

Chapter 5

Cloudy with a Chance of Quail

Before the first raindrop fell, Honi had to have felt a little foolish. Standing inside a circle and demanding rain is risky business. There had to be half a second of doubt. Honi didn't draw a semicircle; he drew a complete circle. There wasn't exactly a way out or an expiration date. Honi backed himself into a circle, and the only way out was a miracle.

Drawing prayer circles often looks like an exercise in foolishness. But that's faith. Faith is the willingness to look foolish. The Israelite army looked foolish marching around Jericho blowing trumpets. Noah looked foolish building a boat in the middle of a desert. David looked foolish charging a giant with a slingshot. The Magi looked foolish following a star to who-knows-where. Peter looked foolish getting out of a boat in the middle of the Sea of Galilee. And Jesus looked foolish wearing a crown of thorns. You get the point, but the results speak for themselves. Noah was saved from the flood; the walls came tumbling down; David defeated Goliath; the Magi discovered the Messiah; Peter walked on water; and Jesus was crowned King of kings.

Foolishness is a feeling that Moses was very familiar with. He had to feel foolish going before Pharaoh and demanding that he let God's people go. He probably felt pretty foolish raising his staff over the Red Sea. And you bet he felt foolish promising meat to eat for the entire nation of Israel in the middle of a desert. Brilliant. But his willingness to look foolish resulted in epic miracles — the exodus of Israel out of Egypt, the parting of the Red Sea, and the quail miracle.

Drawing prayer circles often feels foolish. And the bigger the circle you draw, the more foolish you'll feel. But if you aren't willing to step out of the boat, you'll never walk on water. If you aren't willing to circle the city, the wall will never fall. And if you aren't willing to follow the star, you'll miss out on the greatest adventure of your life!

In order to experience a miracle, you have to take a risk. And one of the most difficult types of risks to take is risking your reputation. Honi already had a reputation as a rainmaker, but he was willing to risk his reputation by praying for rain one more time. Honi took the risk — and the rest is history.

Someone once said that youth wasn't made for fun, it was made for heroism. And heroism always involves risk. In fact, the greatest chapters in history always begin with a risk, and the same is true with the chapters of your life. There comes a moment when you need to make a call, make a decision, or make the move. Circle makers are risk takers.

Moses had learned this lesson well: If you don't take the risk, you forfeit the miracle.

Food Miracles

I love miracles, and I love food, so I *really* love food miracles. And while there are multiple food miracles in Scripture, the day God provided quail meat in the middle of nowhere may rank as the most amazing. When the Israelites exited Egypt, a quailstorm was definitely *not* in the forecast.

> The people of Israel also began to complain, "Oh, for some meat!" they exclaimed. "We remember the fish we used to eat for free in Egypt. And we had all the cucumbers, melons, leeks, onions, and garlic we wanted. But now our appetites are gone. All we ever see is this manna!"[1]

The Israelites were complaining. I know, shocking! Instead of manna, they want meat to eat. And as a hardcore carnivore, I understand that. If you haven't eaten at an all-you-can-eat Brazilian steakhouse, you aren't ready to die yet. But talk about selective memory! They can only remember the free fish they ate in Egypt, and forget the little fact that the food was free because they weren't. The Israelites weren't just slaves; they had been the victims of genocide. Yet they missed the meat on the menu? And isn't it just a little ironic that the Israelites were complaining about one miracle while asking for another one? Their capacity for complaining was pretty outrageous. And we scoff at the Israelites for whining about a meal of manna that was miraculously delivered to their doorsteps every day, but don't we do the same thing? Just listen to the words of those in your school hallway or read the posts on your friend's wall venting about their utterly disastrous life. Watch your parents argue daily over money, worrying about the provision necessary for your family's needs.

There are miracles all around us all the time, yet it's so easy to find something to complain about in the middle of those miracles. The simple act of reading this involves millions of impulses firing across billions of synapses. While you're reading, your heart goes about its business circulating five quarts of blood through a hundred thousand miles of veins, arteries, and capillaries. And it's amazing you can even concentrate, given the fact that you're on a planet that is traveling 67,000 miles per hour through space while spinning around its axis at about 1,000 miles per hour. But we take those manna miracles, the miracles that happen day in, day out, for granted.

Pull an Adam Taylor

Despite the Israelites' incessant complaining, God patiently responds to their food tantrum with one of the most unfathomable promises in Scripture. He doesn't just promise a one-course meal of meat; God promises meat for a month. And Moses can hardly believe it.

> *"Here I am among six hundred thousand men on foot, and you say, 'I will give them meat to eat for a whole month!' Would they have enough if flocks and herds were slaughtered for them? Would they have enough if all the fish in the sea were caught for them?"*[2]

Moses is doing the math in his mind, and it doesn't add up. Not even close! He is trying to think of any conceivable way that God could fulfill this promise, and he can't think of a single scenario. He doesn't see how God can fulfill His impossible promise for a day, let alone a month.

Have you ever been there?

You know God wants you to go on the mission trip, but it doesn't add up. You know God wants you to make some friendship changes, but relationally, it doesn't add up. You know you're supposed to make a difference, but with your resources, it just doesn't add up.

A couple years ago, Adam Taylor went on one of our annual mission trips to Ethiopia. While he was there, he knew God was calling him to invest more than one week of his life. God was calling him to go all in. The defining moment was when a fifteen-year-old boy named Lilly popped out of a sewer manhole cover. He didn't have any shoes on, so Adam spontaneously gave him his. Lilly took Adam on a tour of the sewer, where he found an entire community of orphans living under the streets. In that moment, Adam knew that Ethiopia was his Jericho.

The prospect of leaving a six-digit salary didn't add up, but Adam didn't care. He moved to Addis Ababa, Ethiopia, trusting that God would provide, and he started a ministry called Change Boys, which rescues street kids and gives them a home to live in. In fact, twenty-two kids live with Adam in a house that God miraculously provided. Adam signed the lease on the house, not knowing how God would provide. Meanwhile, we released our annual Christmas catalog that raises money for a variety of mission projects. Adam didn't know it, but Change Boys was one of those projects. How appropriate that Adam's spiritual family at NCC would cover an entire year's lease. When Adam heard the news, he cried. Then we cried. Sometimes crying is the cool thing, the right thing, the only thing you can do.

Adam's story has inspired others within our church to step out in faith too. In fact, his name has been turned into a verb. "Pulling an Adam Taylor" has become synonymous with taking a step of faith that doesn't add up.

Impossible Promises

Meat for a month seems like an impossible promise. And Moses has to decide whether or not he is going to circle it. Logic is screaming no; faith is whispering yes. And Moses has to choose between the two.

This predicament reminds me of another food miracle that happened in the Judean wilderness about fifteen hundred years later. A crowd of five thousand is listening to Jesus speak. He doesn't want to send them away hungry, but there aren't any eating establishments anywhere. Then a nameless boy offers his brown-bag lunch to Jesus. It's a nice gesture, but Andrew just comes out and says what all the other disciples must have been thinking: "How far will they go among so many?"[3] Translation: *Why even offer?* Like Moses, Andrew starts doing the math in his head, and it doesn't add up.

We all learned back in first grade that $5 + 2 = 7$. But if you add God into the equation, $5 + 2 \neq 7$. When you give what you have to God, He multiplies it so that $5 + 2 = 5,000$. Not only does God multiply the meal so that it feeds five thousand; the disciples actually end up with more leftovers than they had food to begin with. Only in God's economy! The twelve baskets of remainders means the most accurate equation is this: $5 + 2 = 5,000$ R12. (End of elementary school flashback, I promise.)

If you put what little you have in your hand into the hand of God, it won't just add up; God will make it multiply.

One footnote.

Do you recall what Jesus did right before the miracle? It says Jesus "gave thanks." He didn't wait until *after* the miracle; He thanked God for the miracle *before* the miracle happened. Jesus put the Jericho principle into practice by praising God before the miracle even happened, as if it had already happened, because He knew His Father would keep His promise. He didn't just pray through; He praised through. What better proof of the concept?

This Is Crazy

You are only one defining decision away from a totally different life. One defining decision can change your trajectory and put you on a new path toward the Promised Land. One defining decision can totally change the forecast of your life. And it's those defining decisions that become the defining moments of our lives.

The quail promise was one of those defining moments for Moses. He had a defining decision to make: to circle or not to circle.

What do you do when the will of God doesn't add up? What do you do when a dream doesn't fit within the logical boundaries of your left brain? What do you do with a promise that seems impossible? What do you do when faith seems foolish?

So Moses went out and told the people what the LORD had said.[4]

Moses risked his reputation and circled the promise. He pushed all of his credibility chips to the middle of the table and told the Israelites that God was going to give them meat for a month. This had to be one of the toughest decisions he ever made, one of the scariest sermons he ever preached. It doesn't add up, but the will of God never does add up by human calculation. Moses had no earthly idea how God was going to keep His promise, but that isn't our business anyway. That is God's business. Too often we let *how* get in the way of *what* God wants us to do. We can't figure out how to do what God has called us to do, so we don't do it at all.

This is what I've come to call a "this is crazy" moment. If we had the transcript of Moses' thoughts, I wonder if it would read, *This is crazy, this is crazy, this is crazy.*

I had one of those "this is crazy" moments last summer while traveling in Peru. After hiking the Inca Trail to Machu Picchu, Parker and I checked a goal off our life goal lists by paragliding over the Sacred Valley. Paragliding is one of those experiences that sounds amazing when your feet are firmly planted on *ground*, but the closer you get to the cliff the more you wonder whether you should be running off it. I have a minor fear of heights, and that fear was not alleviated by the sixty-second orientation given in broken English by my Peruvian tandem partner, who was half my height. His instructions? *Run as fast as you can toward the cliff.* That's it.

As I sprinted toward the ten-thousand-foot drop-off, one thought kept going through my mind: *This is crazy, this is crazy, this is crazy!* But it was quickly followed by, *This is awesome, this is awesome, this is awesome!*

We ran off the cliff and caught an updraft in our parachute. The next thing I knew we were sailing over the Sacred Valley at 14,000 feet. Despite the fact that I lost my lunch seven times in twenty minutes, paragliding ranks as one of the most exhilarating experiences of my life. I learned that if you aren't willing to put yourself in "this is crazy" situations, you'll never experience "this is awesome" moments. If you aren't willing to run off the cliff, you'll never fly. I also learned that paragliding is amazing for your prayer life. You can't *not* pray when you are running off a cliff.

The Law of Measures

While it's not recorded in Scripture, I promise you that Moses prayed. Isn't that what we do when we can't figure things out ourselves? When we find ourselves in situations that are beyond our control or beyond our comprehension, we pray. Moses must have felt like he was running off a cliff, but that is how the parachute of God's promises opens up. It often seems like circling the promises of God is risky, but it's not nearly as risky as *not* circling the promises of God. The greatest risk is failing to circle the promises of God because we forfeit the miracles God wants to perform.

One of the defining moments in the history of NCC was the day we made a defining decision to start giving to missions. We weren't even a self-supporting church at the time, but I felt like God was prompting us to start giving. Have you ever felt like God has called you to do something, but after a quick calculation, you assume the Omniscient One miscalculated? I felt like God was asking us to give what we didn't have, but then I remembered making my first Faith Promise to missions when I was a teenager. I pledged to give fifty dollars to missions despite the fact that I was making minimum wage working at a gas station. I had no idea how I'd be able to fulfill my promise, but God was faithful. I didn't let age keep me from stepping out in faith then and I'm not going to start now. No matter how young or how old someone is, age is never a valid excuse when it comes to doing God's will.

For future reference, arguing with God isn't a good idea. Sure, you can be totally honest with your thoughts and feelings. And I promise that God can take whatever you dish out. But here is what I have learned about arguments with God: If you win the argument you actually lose, and if you lose the argument, you actually win!

I lost the argument, and God won the day. We wrote a $50 check to missions, and what happened next doesn't add up. The next month, our monthly giving tripled from $2,000 to $6,000 and we never looked back. My only explanation is that Luke 6:38 is true. And when we circled this promise by writing that check, God multiplied His provision.

"Give, and it will be given to you. A good measure, pressed down, shaken together and running over, will be poured into your lap. For with the measure you use, it will be measured to you."

I believe in this law of measures. If you give big, God will bless big. That doesn't mean that you can play God like a slot machine, but if you give for the right reasons, I'm convinced of this: *You'll never out-give God.* It's not possible, because God has promised that in the grand scheme of eternity He will always give back more than you gave up.

Last year we gave more than a million dollars to missionaries, but that $50 check still ranks as the hardest and largest gift we've ever given to missions. It didn't add up, but God made it multiply. And He'll do the same for you. You have to respond to His nudge to go from "this is crazy" to "this is awesome." When you live in obedience, you position yourself for blessing. And you never know how or when or where God is going to show up. He might just send winds out of the west at fifty miles per hour with a 100 percent chance of quail.

Quailmageddon

Now a wind went out from the LORD and drove quail in from the sea. It scattered them up to two cubits deep all around the camp, as far as a day's walk in any direction. All that day and night and all the next day the people went out and gathered quail. No one gathered less than ten homers.[5]

The Israelites were parked in the Desert of Paran, a region about fifty miles inland from the Mediterranean Sea and fifty miles southwest of the Dead Sea. The significance is this: Quail tend to live by the water, and they don't fly long distances. If it hadn't been for a little super-natural wind, they would have never made it this far inland. So this is a meteorological miracle. And it's not just a miraculous west wind. The clouds burst and rained quail from the sky.

When quail get tired, they dive-bomb. We're not talking about a perfectly angled duck that makes a smooth landing on a watery run-way; quail were falling from the sky like huge pieces of hail. There had to be more than one black eye as the Israelites looked up to see quail falling from the sky. Then they ran for cover! Scripture also says that some of the quail flew into the camp about three feet off the ground, so there may have been some below-the-belt bruises as well.

Based on the Hebrew system of measurement, "a day's walk" would be like fifteen miles in any direction. So drawing on your geometry classes, if you square the radius and multiply by *pi*, we're talking about an area that was almost 700 square miles. To put that into perspective, Washington, DC, is 68.3 square miles. Not only was this an area ten times larger than the nation's capital, but the quail were piled three feet deep as well. Who knew there were even that many quail on earth?

Can you imagine seeing that many birds fly into the camp? It was like a bird blizzard. Quailmageddon. The cloud of birds was so mas-sive that it seemed like a solar eclipse. For the rest of their lives, when the eyewitnesses who were there that day closed their eyes at night, they counted quail.

Once the quail stopped falling, the Israelites started gathering. Each Israelite gathered no less than ten homers. Ten homers mul-tiplied by 600,000 men equals 6 million homers at a minimum. A homer equated to roughly 200 liters, and assuming that the quail were of an average size, it rained somewhere in the neighborhood of 105 million quail. You read that right: *105 million quail*. God doesn't just provide in dramatic fashion; God provides in dramatic proportion.

One of the reasons I love this miracle is because it's something of a miracle pun. This miracle is recorded in the book of Numbers, and the Greek name for Numbers is *arithmoi*, where we get our word *arithmetic*. So recorded in the book of arithmetic is a miracle that doesn't even begin to add up.

Moses could never have anticipated this answer to prayer. It was unpredictable and unprecedented, but Moses had the guts to circle the promise anyway! And when you circle the promise, you never know how God will provide, but it's always cloudy with a chance of quail.

Do you think that perhaps you need to quit doing arithmetic and start doing geometry? When God enters the equation, His output always exceeds your input. Your only job is to draw circles in the sand. And if you do the geometry, God will multiply the miracles in your life.

Draw the Circle

1. God often tells us to do crazy things that just don't add up. Have you ever had a "this is crazy" moment that turned into "this is awesome"? Have you ever risked your reputation for God? How?

2. Do you know anyone who has pulled an Adam Taylor? How did they step out in faith?

3. One defining decision can change the entire direction of your life and forecast your future. What might that defining decision be in your life right now?

Chapter 6

You Can't Never Always Sometimes Tell

I almost said no to a miracle once.

A couple who had just started attending our church requested a meeting, and I came close to denying the request because they said they wanted to talk about church government. I *love* talking about the mission and vision of the church. Church government? Not as much! Plus, I was fighting a book deadline, so I didn't have much extra time in my schedule. So I almost said no, and if I had, I would have missed out on a miracle.

As we sat in my office above Ebenezer's Coffeehouse (which our church owns), they peppered me with questions about bylaws, financial checks and balances, and decision-making protocols. And while I felt a little defensive at the time, I realize now that they were simply doing their due diligence. Like investors who research a company before purchasing stock (if you don't already, you'll know all about that in a few years), they wanted to make sure it would be a good return on investment. After answering nearly ninety minutes worth of questions, they ended by asking me about our vision. I had so much pent-up passion after talking about policies and protocols that I just let it rip. I shared our vision of starting a Dream Center in Ward 8, the poorest part of our city and the primary reason the nation's capital is always in the running for murder capital of the country. I talked about turning our coffeehouse on Capitol Hill into a chain of coffeehouses, with all the net profits reinvested in missions. I talked about launching our first international campus in Berlin, Germany. And I shared our vision of launching multisite campuses in movie theaters at metro stops throughout the greater Washington area. Then the meeting came to a rather abrupt and awkward ending. They said they wanted to invest in National Community Church, but they didn't say how or how much. They left, and I was left scratching my head.

I wasn't sure anything would come of that meeting, but a few weeks later, they asked my assistant for a phone appointment. On an otherwise uneventful Wednesday afternoon, right around three o'clock, I received one of the most unforgettable phone calls of my life.

"Pastor Mark, we wanted to follow up on our meeting and let you know that we want to give a gift to National Community Church."

My mind immediately started racing.

Our congregation is amazingly generous, but most people are right around twenty-eight and nearly two-thirds of our congregation are single, which means that most of our attendees are nowhere near their peak earning potential. They tithe on their income as Hill staffers or inner-city schoolteachers or coffeehouse baristas, but they don't have the income or savings to give large financial gifts. They're going to be more focused on paying off school loans or saving for a wedding.

The largest single gift we had ever received up to that point was a $42,000 tithe on the sale of a home, but I couldn't help but wonder if this gift might exceed that gift. After all, you don't announce a gift if it isn't a gift worth announcing, right?

"We want to give a gift, and there are no strings attached. But before I tell you how much we're going to give, I want you to know why we're giving it. We're giving this gift because you have vision beyond your resources." I'll never forget that.

The thought behind the gift was just as meaningful as the gift itself. And that thought has inspired us to keep dreaming irrational dreams. Those four words, *vision beyond your resources*, have become a mantra for the ministry of NCC. We refuse to let our budget determine our vision. That left-brained approach is a wrong-brained approach because it's based on our limited resources rather than on God's unlimited provision! Faith is allowing your God-given vision to determine what is possible. That certainly does *not* mean you practice poor financial stewardship, spend beyond your means, and build up a huge debt load, or even take risks carelessly. It does mean that you take a step of faith when God gives you a vision because you trust that the One who gave you the vision is going to make provision. And for the record, if the vision is from God, it will most definitely be beyond your means.

Having vision beyond your resources is synonymous with dreaming big. And it may feel like you're setting yourself up for failure, but you're really setting God up for a miracle. How God performs the miracle is His job. Your job is drawing a circle around the God-given dream. And if you do your job, you might just find yourself standing waist-deep in three feet of quail.

"We want to give the church $3 million."

I was speechless. And I'm a preacher.

I heard it, but was having a *really* hard time believing it. I was blindsided by the blessing. Like the wind that brought 105 million quail into the camp, God's provision came out of nowhere.

It's not our man-made plans that move the Almighty; the Almighty is moved by big dreams and bold prayers. In the awkward silence of my speechlessness, I heard the still, small voice of the Spirit. The Holy Spirit hit the rewind button and reminded me of a prayer circle that I had drawn four years before.

Let me retrace the circle.

Prayer Promise

On March 15, 2006, we opened the doors to our coffeehouse on Capitol Hill. The total cost of building Ebenezer's Coffeehouse was over $3 million, and our mortgage was $2 million. One day, I was praying for God's provision when I felt a prompting to pray for a $2 million miracle. The first thing I had to do was decipher whether this prompting was just my own desire to be debt free or whether it was the Holy Spirit who dropped that promise into my heart. It's tough to discern between natural desires and holy desires, but I was about 90 percent sure it was the Holy Spirit who put that promise in my heart. I had no idea how God would do it, but I knew I needed to circle that promise in prayer.

I mentioned this $2 million miracle to a few circle makers, who started praying with me for God's provision. There were certainly weeks and months when I failed to even think or pray about the promise, but we circled that $2 million promise off and on for four years.

About a year after God gave me that prayer promise, I got what I thought was a $2 million idea for an online company called GodiPod. com. My wife and I invested the money to get the business off the ground, but that $2 million idea turned out to be a $15,000 personal loss. Looking back, I think I was trying to manufacture the miracle for God. We do this so often, don't we? When God doesn't answer our prayer right away, we try to answer it for Him. Moses took matters into his own hands and killed an Egyptian taskmaster, and we do the same thing (minus the killing part). We get ahead of God. But when we try to do God's job for Him, it's going to backfire. Trying to get ahead of God cost Moses forty years. Of course, even then, God redeemed the forty years Moses spent as a fugitive tending sheep by prepping him to tend His sheep, the people of Israel. God always recycles our mistakes.

One important lesson I've learned is that no doesn't always mean no; sometimes no means not yet. Go back and read that one more time. We're too quick to give up on God when He doesn't answer our prayers when we want or how we want. Maybe your deadline doesn't fit God's timeline. Maybe no simply means not yet. It might just be a divine delay.

One other lesson: you shouldn't seek answers as much as you should seek God. We get overanxious. We're constantly looking for clues about our future, our dating life, what college we'll go to, and the list goes on. We try to microwave our own answers instead of trusting God's timing. But here's an important reminder: If you go looking for answers, you won't find them, but if you seek God, answers will just naturally find you. There comes a point after you have prayed through that you need to let go and let God. How? By resisting the temptation to manufacture your own answer to your own prayer.

It would have been easy to cash out on the $2 million promise after GodiPod.com failed, but I kept circling that promise. I wouldn't have guessed that the payoff would happen in a meeting about church government, of all things. But I quit trying to manufacture my own answer and simply trusted that God would give an answer when I was ready for it. Then one afternoon, right around three o'clock, God came out of nowhere and delivered on His promise with a holy surprise.

The Element of Surprise

Our family has a handful of sayings that have been passed down from generation to generation. I bet yours does too if you stop and think about what gets said over and over again. Those sayings become part of your family folklore, don't they? I'm not sure where this one originated, but I remember my grandma repeating it more than once: *You can't never always sometimes tell.* That tongue twister is a mind-bender, so you might need to read it twice. Here's a translation: "Anything could happen."

Let me redeem that saying and give it a prayer twist. When you circle a promise in prayer, *you can't never always sometimes tell.* Anything could happen! You simply never know when or how or where God will answer it. Prayer adds an element of surprise to your life (and this is even better than a surprise party or surprise gift or surprise romance, believe me). In fact, prayer turns life into a party, a gift, *and* a romance.

God has surprised me so many times that I'm not even surprised by His surprises anymore. That doesn't mean I love them any less. I'm in awe of the strange and mysterious ways in which God works, but I've sort of come to expect the unexpected because God is predictably unpredictable. God always has a holy surprise up His sovereign sleeve! The only thing I can predict with absolute certainty is this: the more you pray the more holy surprises will happen.

I recently spoke at an NFL chapel. I've done a few of them, but this one was special because it was *my team.* Not only that, my all-time favorite player whose *signed* jersey I wear on *every single* game day was there. And I'll be honest, I was a little nervous. There is something about speaking to very large men who paint their faces, put on helmets, and inflict pain upon one another that's a little intimidating. And the team sack leader was in the front row!

I preached my heart out that night because, quite frankly, I wanted them to win the next day! But I also knew it was a divine appointment, and I felt a unique anointing. There was a reason that God would choose a die-hard fan to speak to the team. Afterward I shook hands with the guys, and I thought that was that, but *you can't never always sometimes tell.* After the season was over, I had dinner with the guy I had cheered for during his entire career. Afterward we were standing in the parking lot of the restaurant, and I couldn't help but chuckle. I told him that I had prayed for him a thousand times, but every prayer was focused on football. That night I prayed for *him.* Not the football player. The person. That's just like God, isn't it? When you draw a prayer circle, even if that circle is limited by your ignorance, you never know how or when or where God will answer it. One prayer leads to another, which leads to another, and where they will take you no one knows, except the One who knows all.

Over the past year, I've been repeating one prayer with great frequency: "Lord, do something unpredictable and uncontrollable."

That's a scary prayer, especially for a control freak like me, but not nearly as much as a life without lots of holy surprises. And you can't have it both ways. If you want God to surprise you, you have to give up control. You will lose a measure of predictability, but you'll begin to see God move in uncontrollable ways!

Anything could happen. Anyplace. Anytime.

It's the only way to live!

One Afternoon

I believe that God inspires every word of Scripture. And while chapters like Psalm 23 or verses like John 3:16 top the memorization charts, there are also moments when the same Holy Spirit who inspired the writers of Scripture will inspire the readers of Scripture with an unlikely nudge. Some word or phrase will jump off the page and get into your spirit. One of those unlikely inspirations happened as I was reading Acts 10:3:

One day at about three in the afternoon he had a vision.[1]

Here's the context. There was a Roman captain named Cornelius who gave generously to the poor and "prayed to God regularly."[2] That prayer habit kept him in tune with God and set the stage for this vision. At this point, Christianity was just a branch of Judaism, but this vision changes the course of Christianity because the gospel is opened up to the Gentiles (in other words, the non-Jews) for the first time.

"One day at about three in the afternoon." Three in the afternoon. How odd! But that's what I love about it. When you pray regularly, you never know when God will show up or speak up, and today could be the day. When you live in prayer mode, you live with holy anticipation. What does that mean? You know that coincidences are providences. Any moment can turn into your moment. God can invade the reality of your life at three o'clock one afternoon, right after school, at the bus stop or in the parking lot, and change everything.

Perplex Me

One of the biggest surprises in Scripture happened on the day of Pentecost. No one could have scripted that miracle. Peter got up bright and early, but had literally no idea that God would pour out His Spirit like flames of fire or that the believers would spontaneously speak in the languages they had never learned or that they would baptize three thousand people before the day was done. It was unpredictable and uncontrollable. Yet how appropriate that this holy surprise happens on the birthday of the church. God threw a surprise party! And God knows how to party!

Scripture says the people were "amazed and perplexed."[3] All of us want to be amazed by God, right? It's easy to pray, "Amaze me!" Though I don't know anyone who prays, "Perplex me!" But it's a package deal. If you aren't willing to be perplexed, you'll never be amazed.

Cornelius had a vision one day at three in the afternoon. The next afternoon, around noon, Peter had a perplexing vision while praying on the rooftop of Simon the tanner's house. He saw a huge blanket filled with animals, like reptiles and birds, and the Lord said to Peter, "Kill and eat." You've got to love Peter's response:

"Surely not, Lord!"[4]

That deserves a pause. If Jesus truly is Lord, then I don't think you're allowed to say *surely not*. No is not an option. Yet Peter thinks God has misspoken or he had misheard. But before you criticize Peter, realize that we often do the same thing when God gives us a dream that is beyond our ability to comprehend.

Peter has a hard time processing this perplexing vision. And he wasn't just perplexed. He was "very perplexed."[5] Why? Because the vision was in direct violation of Jewish dietary laws, which forbade the eating of unclean animals. What God was asking went against everything Peter had ever been taught. Peter says, "I have never eaten anything impure or unclean."[6] So God in His endless patience repeats the vision three times. That must've been Peter's magic number. And the third time was the charm.

It's in these times where God wants to do something unprecedented that many of us get stuck spiritually. Instead of operating by faith, we switch back to our default logic setting. Instead of embracing the new move of God, we fall back on old routines.

Peter was perplexed by this vision, but he took a step of faith. He risked his reputation by breaking every law in the Jewish books and stepping foot into Cornelius's house. It was crazy because it was considered unclean, but that one small step proved to be a giant leap. That doorframe was something of a wormhole. The split second that Peter crossed that threshold, all Gentiles were given complete access to the gospel. If you aren't Jewish, your spiritual genealogy traces back to this moment. Peter had the faith to cross the chasm because he circled a perplexing vision in prayer. Every Gentile who comes to faith in Jesus Christ is an answer to the prayer circle that Peter drew one afternoon on the rooftop of Simon the tanner's house.

Are you willing to be perplexed? Are you open to holy surprises? Do you have the courage for God to move in unpredictable and uncontrollable ways?

If you aren't open to the unprecedented, well, you'll just repeat history. If you *are* open to the unprecedented, you will change history. The only difference is prayer.

The Brown Grocery-Paper Vision

Hattie was born into the most distinguished family of clergymen in America. Her father, Lyman Beecher, was considered the greatest speaker in America. That mantle was passed down to her brother, Henry Ward Beecher. But it was Hattie who would actually *change* the course of American history.

One Sunday morning in 1851, during a Communion service, Harriet fell into a trance not unlike the trance that Peter had on the rooftop of Simon the tanner's house. In her trance, Hattie saw an old slave being beaten to death. The vision left her so shaken that she could hardly keep from weeping. She walked her children home from church and skipped lunch. She immediately started writing down the vision God had given her as words poured from her pen. When she ran out of paper, she found brown grocery paper and continued to write. When she finally stopped, and read what she wrote, she could hardly believe she had written it. It was nothing short of divine inspiration. Hattie said that God wrote the book; she just put the words on paper.

In January 1852, a year after Harriet Beecher Stowe's vision, the forty-five-chapter manuscript of *Uncle Tom's Cabin* was ready for publication. Yup. *Uncle Tom's Cabin* from US History, 3rd period. The publisher, John P. Jewett, didn't think the book would sell many copies, but three thousand copies were sold the first day. The entire first printing was sold out by the end of the second day. The third and fourth printings were sold out before the book was even reviewed. The book that Jewett didn't think would sell many copies ended up in almost every house in America, including the White House. No novel has had a greater effect on the conscience of a country than Harriet Beecher Stowe's vision, *Uncle Tom's Cabin*. In fact, when Hattie met President Lincoln, he said: "So you're the little woman who started this Great War!"

Never underestimate the power of a single prayer. God can do anything through anyone who circles their big dreams with bold prayers. With God, there is no precedent, because all things are possible. Providing meat for a month in the middle of nowhere is no problem when you own the cattle on the thousand hills. God can use the bold prayer of a sage to end a drought or the bold pen of a young mother to end slavery. If you have the courage to circle the dream in prayer, *you can't never always sometimes tell.*

Praystorm

I believe in planning. Failing to plan is planning to fail. But I also believe this: One bold prayer can accomplish more than a thousand well-laid plans. So go ahead and plan, but make sure you circle your plans in prayer. If your plans aren't soaked with prayer, they won't succeed. This much I know from personal experience. When I was twenty-two and planting a church in Chicago, I had a twenty-five-year plan. That "well-laid" plan was a project for one of my seminary classes, and I actually got an *A* on it. In reality, I should have gotten an *F* because it failed. I still have that twenty-five-year plan in my files.

Few things sting more than a failed plan, but I've always drawn a little bit of humor and humility from the old saying, "If you want to make God laugh, tell him your plans." It's not a vindictive chuckle, as if God enjoys our failure. I just think God is sometimes amazed at how small our plans are. He allows our small plans to fail so that His big dream for us can prevail. The glass is half full, my friends! So keep planning like it depends on you, but make sure you pray like it depends on God. Prayer is the alpha and omega, the beginning and the end, of planning. Don't just brainstorm; praystorm.

You can't never always sometimes tell.

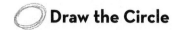 **Draw the Circle**

1. Think of a time when it seemed as if God was silent — that He didn't answer your prayer as you asked, or at least not in the timeframe or way you hoped. How did you respond? What did this show you about yourself? What did it show you about God?

2. Is it possible for a spiritually mature person to pray the wrong things for the wrong reasons? Explain. Have you prayed the wrong things for the wrong reasons?

3. If you seek answers, you won't find them, but if you seek God, the answers will find you. How have you found this to be true in your life? Why is it important to seek God above any answer to prayer? How might our relationship with Him change if we did this?

Chapter 7

The Solution to
Ten Thousand Problems

Before the quailstorm showed up on radar, God asks Moses a question. It's more than *a* question; it's *the* question. Your answer to this question, *the question*, will determine the size of your prayer circles.

"Is there a limit to my power?"[1]

The obvious answer to that question is "No, Lord!" God is omnipotent, which means by definition, there's nothing God can't do. Yet many of us pray as if our problems are bigger than God. So let me remind you of this high-octane truth that should fuel your faith: God is infinitely bigger than your biggest problem or biggest dream. And while we're on the topic, His grace is infinitely bigger than your biggest sin.

It's our low view of God that is the cause of all lesser problems and it's a high view of God that is the solution. Your biggest problem isn't a broken relationship, your parents' divorce, or a bad grade. Please understand, I'm not making light of your dating, family, or academic issues. I certainly don't want to minimize the overwhelming challenges you may be facing. But in order to obtain a godly perspective on your problems, you have to answer this question: Are your problems bigger than God, or is God bigger than your problems? Our biggest problem is our low view of God. That is the cause of all lesser sins. And it's a high view of God that is the solution to all other problems.

Is there a limit to my power?

Have you answered *the question*? It's a big deal and there are only two options: yes or no. Once you embrace the unlimited power of God, you'll draw bigger and bigger circles around your God-given, God-sized dreams.

How big is your God? Is He big enough to help you find the right person for your future or heal your broken family? Is He bigger than a bad grade or a bad game? Is He bigger than your secret sin or secret dream?

Sizing Up God

Moses was perplexed by the promise God had given him. (What a great word: *perplexed*.) How could God possibly provide meat for a month? It didn't add up! But at that critical intersection, when Moses had to decide whether or not to circle the promise, God popped *the question*.

Is there a limit to my power?

When God prompted me to pray for a $2 million miracle, I had to answer *the question*. It seemed like an impossible promise to me, but to the God who can provide 105 million quail out of nowhere, what's $2 million?

The size of our prayers depends on the size of our God. And if God knows no limits, then neither should our prayers. God exists outside of the four space-time dimensions He created. We should pray that way!

It reminds me of the man who was sizing up God by asking, "God, how long is a million years to you?" God said, "A million years is like a second." Then the man asked, "How much is a million dollars to you?" God said, "A million dollars is like a penny." The man smiled and said, "Could you spare a penny?" God smiled back and said, "Sure, just wait a second."

No worries, the jokes get better. Keep reading.

With God, there is no big or small, easy or difficult, possible or impossible. This is difficult to comprehend because all we've ever known are the four dimensions we were born into, but God isn't subject to the laws of nature that He created. He has no beginning and no end. To the infinite, all finites are equal. Even our hardest prayers are easy for God to answer because there is no degree of difficulty.

If you're like me, you tend to use bigger words for bigger requests. You pull out your best vocabulary words for your biggest prayers, as if God's answer depends on the correct combination of words. Trust me, it doesn't matter how long or how loud you pray; it comes down to your answer to *the question*.

Is there a limit to my power?

With God, it's never an issue of "Can He?" It's only a question of "Will He?" And while you don't always know if He *will*, you should always know that He *can*. And because you know He can, you can pray with holy confidence.

Warts

I answered *the question* when I was thirteen years old, or maybe I should say, *the question* was answered for me. Our family visited a new church one Sunday, and a prayer team from that church showed up unannounced at our front door on Monday. The doorbell caught us a little off guard. So did their faith. After introducing themselves, they simply asked if we needed prayer for anything. At that point in my life, I struggled with severe asthma. I was hospitalized half a dozen times during my preteen years. So we asked them to ask God to heal me. That prayer team formed a prayer circle around me and laid their hands on my head. It made me feel a little awkward, but I had never heard anyone pray with that much intensity. They prayed as if they believed. And then they left.

Sometime while I was sleeping that night, God did a miracle, but it wasn't exactly the miracle I expected. God answered a prayer, but it wasn't really the answer I anticipated. I still had asthma the next morning, but every wart on my feet was gone. No kidding. At first I wondered if this was some kind of prayer joke, or if God misinterpreted the prayer. Like prayer is like the old game of telephone, and somewhere between here and heaven asthma got translated into warts. Maybe there was someone with warts who was breathing great that day because they got my answer while I got theirs.

That's when I heard the still, small voice of the Holy Spirit for the first time in my life. Please understand that Spirit-whispers aren't all that common, but those whispers echo forever. The Spirit said to my spirit, *Mark, I just want you to know that I'm able.*

Like the day after *the day* God sent rain in answer to Honi's prayer, it was hard *not* to believe the next day. Once you experience a miracle, there's no turning back. It's difficult to doubt God after that. I wonder if that was how Moses was able to circle the impossible promise of meat to eat. God had already sent manna. God had already parted the Red Sea. God had already performed ten miraculous signs and delivered Israel out of Egypt. How can you *not* believe when God has proven Himself over and over again?

One footnote.

This question — Is there a limit to my power? — is translated differently in different versions of the Bible. One version reads, "Is the LORD's arm too short?" Another translation reads, "Is the LORD's hand waxed short?" [2] In both instances, the hand or arm of the Lord is referenced as a metaphor for God's power.

With that context, look back at the ten miracles God performed to deliver Israel out of Egypt. These miracles are not attributed to the hand of God or arm of God.

"This is the finger of God." [3]

Wow. While we don't know which finger it was, those ten miracles were attributed to one finger. Which one? My guess is it was His pinky! And if one finger is capable of ten miracles, then what can the hand of God or entire *arm* of God accomplish?

When it comes to the will of God, I strike out all the time. And my prayer batting average is no better than anyone else when it comes to hitting God's curveballs. (The prayer puns get better too.) I often second-guess the will of God, but I don't doubt the power of God. God is able. I don't always know if He will, but I always know that He can.

15.5 Billion Light-Years

While God's power is technically measureless, the prophet Isaiah gives us a glimpse of God's omnipotence by comparing it to the size of the universe. The distance between His wisdom and ours, His power and ours, is likened to the distance from one side of the universe to the other.

As the heavens are higher than the earth,
so are my ways higher than your ways
and my thoughts than your thoughts.[4]

The universe is larger than we can imagine, but let me try to put it into perspective. The basic unit of measurement is a light-year. Light travels at 186,000 miles per second, which is so fast that in the time it takes to snap your fingers, light circles the globe half a dozen times. (You just snapped your fingers, didn't you?) The sun is 94.4 million miles away from the earth at its farthest distance from us. If you could drive to the sun traveling 65 miles per hour, 24 hours a day, 365 days a year, it would take you more than 163 years to get there. The light that warms your face on a sunny day, on the other hand, left the surface of the sun only *8 minutes ago*. So while 94.4 million miles may seem like a long distance by earthly standards, it's our next-door neighbor by astronomical measurements. The sun's the nearest star in our tiny little galaxy known as the Milky Way. There are more than 80 billion galaxies in the universe, which, for the record, equates to more than 10 galaxies per person! I don't think you have to worry about running out of things to do when you get to heaven. It's an awfully big sandbox.

In one minute, light travels 11 million miles. In one day, light travels 160 billion miles. In one year, light travels an unfathomable 5 trillion, 865 billion, 696 million miles. But that's just one light-year. The outer edge of the universe, according to astrophysicists, is 15.5 billion light-years away! If that seems incomprehensible, it's because it's virtually unimaginable. Yet God says that this is the distance between His thoughts and our thoughts. So here's my thought: Your best thought on your best day falls 15.5 billion light-years short of how great and how good God really is. Even the most brilliant among us underestimate God by 15.5 billion light-years. God is able to do 15.5 billion light-years beyond what you can ask or imagine.

By definition, a big dream is a dream that is bigger than you. In other words, it's beyond your ability to accomplish. And this means there'll be moments when you doubt yourself. That's normal. But that's when you need to remind yourself that your dream isn't bigger than God; God is 15.5 billion light-years bigger than your dream. I hope that gives you a little perspective.

If you've never had a God-sized dream that scared you half to death, then you haven't really come to life. If you've never been overwhelmed by the impossibility of your plans, then your God is too small. If your vision isn't perplexing and impossible, then you need to widen the diameter of your prayer circles.

Called, Not Qualified

A big dream is simultaneously the best feeling and worst feeling in the world. It's exhilarating because it's beyond your ability; it's frightening for the same exact reason. So if you're going to dream big, you have to be able to manage the emotional tension. Facing your fears is the beginning of the battle. Circling them over and over again is the rest of the story.

Have you ever felt like your dream was too big for you?

Moses definitely felt that way more than once. When God called him to lead the Israelites out of Egypt, Moses felt like it might be too big of a task. He felt like he wasn't qualified, so he asked God to send someone else to do it. In my experience, you'll never feel qualified. But, here's another mantra for your arsenal: *God doesn't call the qualified; God qualifies the called.*

I wasn't qualified to pastor National Community Church. The only thing I had on my résumé was a nine-week summer internship. We had zero know-how going into the coffeehouse business. No one on our team had ever worked in a coffeehouse when we started pursuing that dream. But it doesn't matter if you qualify for the job, qualify for the college loan, or qualify for the program. If God has called you, you're qualified.

The issue is never, "Are you qualified?" The issue is always, "Are you called?"

I make this distinction between *qualified* and *called* with aspiring writers all the time. Too many authors worry about whether or not their book will get published. That isn't the question. The question is this: Are you called to write? That's the only question you need to answer. And if the answer is yes, then you need to write the book as an act of obedience. It doesn't matter whether anyone reads it or not. Maybe for you, "writing" is a call to join a club at school or even a feeling you're meant to be a doctor even though you always saw yourself as a musician. You might not be the best debater on the team, and you might find chemistry difficult to pass without a tutor, but if you're called, those details don't matter.

I remember the day I walked into Union Station to do some recon and look into renting the movie theaters for our Sunday services. I felt intimidated by the opportunity. It seemed too good. It seemed too big. We were a church of only fifty people at that point, and Union Station was the most visited destination in Washington, DC. How are fifty people going to hold service in a place where twenty-five million people pass through every year? We barely filled a large living room. How could we fill what was once the largest room under a single roof in the world? The dream was too big for me, but it's never too big for God. And what seemed too big then eventually became too small to contain what God was doing through us.

If you're looking to grow spiritually, you need to keep stretching. How? By going after dreams that are bigger than you are. When NCC was a church of fifty people, we took a huge step of faith by hosting a Convoy of Hope outreach that fed five thousand people. Convoy of Hope is a great organization that literally gives truckloads of food and relief to communities that are in desperate need. We knew it required four hundred volunteers. We knew we only had fifty people. But we felt that God was calling us to go for it.

A few years ago, we hosted another Convoy of Hope at RFK Stadium. This time we fed ten thousand people. I think Jesus would have been proud, even if we used more than five loaves and two fish. As we were recuperating from the huge expenditure of time, energy, and resources, we felt God challenging us: *Why don't you do this every day?* To be honest, we were pretty satisfied doing it once a year, but God upped the ante. Now our dream is a Dream Center in southeast

DC that serves as a need-meeting machine 24/7. It's beyond our ability, and that's exactly why we believe God will bless it.

Occasionally when you hear answers to prayer that others have experienced, it can have a reverse effect and be discouraging instead of encouraging because you wonder why God has answered *their* prayers but not yours. But let me remind you that these answers have rarely happened as quickly or easily as they sound. There is usually a way longer backstory. So while we are quick to celebrate the answer to prayer, the answer probably didn't come quickly. I've never met a person who didn't experience some big disappointments on the way to his or her big dream.

Sometimes the power of prayer is the power to carry on. It doesn't always change your circumstances, but it gives you the strength to walk through them. When you pray through, the burden is taken off of your shoulders and carried by your Savior, who carried the cross to Calvary.

Is your dream too big for you?

It better be, because that will force you to pray circles around it. If you keep circling it in prayer, God will get bigger and bigger until you see your impossible prayer for what it really is: an easy answer for an almighty God.

Draw the Circle

1. Sometimes God seems small to us in the face of our problems because we have forgotten the many ways He has proven Himself to us in the past. How has God shown Himself to be huge in your life? How has God shown Himself to be loving and faithful? What are the good things God has done for you or for the people you know and love? Dwell on these things to see God at His true size.

2. As you consider the vastness of our limitless God, that He is billions of times bigger than any prayer you can pray or dream you can dream, how does this change the way you pray?

3. When have you felt discouraged rather than encouraged after God answered someone else's prayer—perhaps one similar to your own prayer that remains unanswered? At such times, how can you see God as being bigger than that discouragement?

Part 2

The Second Circle — Pray Hard

One day Jesus told his disciples a story to show that they should always pray and never give up. "There was a judge in a certain city," *he said, "who neither feared God nor cared about people. A widow of that city came to him repeatedly, saying, 'Give me justice in this dispute with my enemy.' The judge ignored her for a while, but finally he said to himself, 'I don't fear God or care about people, but this woman is driving me crazy. I'm going to see that she gets justice, because she is wearing me out with her constant requests!'"* [1]

This parable of the persistent widow is one of the most pixilated pictures of prayer in Scripture. It shows us what praying hard looks like: knocking until your knuckles are raw, crying out until your voice is lost, and pleading until you're out of tears. Praying hard is *praying through*. And if you pray through, God will come through. But remember that it will be on God's timeline and in God's way.

There's a phrase used to describe the widow's persistence: "She is wearing me out." That's boxing terminology, and it's appropriate because praying hard sometimes feels like going twelve rounds with God. A heavyweight prayer bout with God Almighty can be excruciating and exhausting, but that is how the greatest prayer victories are won. Praying hard is more than words; it's blood, sweat, and tears. Praying hard is two-dimensional: praying like it depends on God, and working like it depends on you. It's praying until God answers, no matter how long it takes. It's doing whatever it takes to show God you're serious.

Desperate times call for desperate measures, and there is no more desperate act than praying hard. There's going to come a time when you need to throw caution to the wind and draw a circle in the sand. There will come a day when you need to break the rules of decorum, drop to your knees, and pray for the impossible. And there will be a moment when you need to muster every ounce of faith you have and call down rain from heaven. For the persistent widow, this was that moment.

While we don't know what injustice took place, we do know that the persistent widow wouldn't take no for an answer. That's what made her a circle maker. Maybe her son was tossed in prison for a crime he didn't commit. Maybe the man who attacked her daughter was still on the streets. Whatever it was, the judge knew this woman would never give up and that she would circle his house until the day she died if she didn't get justice. The judge knew she wasn't going anywhere.

Can *The Judge* say the same about you?

How desperate are you for the miracle? Desperate enough to pray through the night? How many times are you willing to circle the promise? Until the day you die? How long and loud will you knock on the door of opportunity? Until you knock the door down?

If you aren't desperate, you won't take desperate measures. And if you don't pray like it depends on God, the biggest miracles and best promises will remain out of your prayer reach. But if you learn how to pray hard, like the persistent widow, God will honor your bold prayers because your bold prayers honor God.

Like Honi the circle maker, the persistent widow's methods weren't exactly mainstream. She could have, and technically should have, waited for her court date. Going to the personal residence of the judge crosses a professional line. I'm almost surprised the judge didn't get a restraining order against her. But this reveals something about the nature of God. God couldn't care less about proper procedure or protocol. If He did, Jesus would have chosen the Pharisees as His disciples. But that isn't who Jesus honored. Jesus honored the prostitute who crashed a party at a Pharisee's home in order to anoint His feet. Jesus honored the tax collector who climbed a tree in his three-piece suit just to get a glimpse of Jesus. Jesus honored the four friends who cut in line by cutting a hole in someone's ceiling to help their friend. And in this parable, Jesus honored the woman who drove a judge crazy because she wouldn't stop knocking.

The common denominator in each of these stories is holy desperation. People took desperate measures to get to God, and God honored them for it. Nothing has changed. God is still honoring spiritual desperadoes who crash parties and climb trees. God is still honoring those who defy the way things should be with their bold prayers. God is still honoring those who pray with bravery and stubbornness. And the persistent widow is the gold standard when it comes to praying hard. Her unrelenting persistence was the only difference between justice and injustice.

The power of our prayers doesn't depend on how we put together the twenty-six letters of the English alphabet into the right combination of words like *abracadabra*. God already knows the last punctuation mark before we pronounce the first syllable. The power of our prayers has more to do with intensity than vocabulary. That is modeled by the Holy Spirit Himself. He has been intensely and unceasingly interceding for you your entire life.

Psalm 32:7 is a must-circle promise. I like the King James Version: "Thou shalt compass me about with songs of deliverance."

Long before you woke up this morning and long after you go to sleep tonight, the Spirit of God was circling you with songs of deliverance. He has been circling you since the day you were conceived, and He'll circle you until the day you die. The Holy Spirit is praying hard for you with groans that can't even be translated into any of our human languages.

Chapter 8

Persistence Quotient

In standardized math tests, Japanese kids consistently score higher than their American counterparts. Surprisingly, researchers have discovered that it has more to do with effort than ability. The Japanese kids don't necessarily know more, they just try harder. In a study involving first graders, students were given a difficult puzzle to solve. The researchers weren't interested in whether or not the children could solve the puzzle; they simply wanted to see how long they would try before giving up. The American children lasted, on average, 9.47 minutes. The Japanese children lasted 13.93 minutes. In other words, the Japanese children tried about 40 percent longer.[1] Is it any wonder that they score higher on math exams? Researchers concluded that the difference in math scores might have less to do with intelligence quotient and more to do with persistence quotient. The Japanese first graders simply tried harder.

That study doesn't just explain the difference in math test scores; the implications are true no matter where you turn. It doesn't matter whether it's athletics or academics, music or math. There are no shortcuts. There are no substitutes. You can't be successful without persistence.

Done thinking about that one? Okay. Next study. More than a decade ago, Anders Ericsson and his colleagues at Berlin's elite Academy of Music did a study with musicians. With the help of some professors, they divided violinists into three groups: world-class soloists, good violinists, and those who were unlikely to play professionally. All of them started playing at roughly the same age and practiced about the same amount of time until the age of eight. That's when their practice habits went in different directions. The researchers found that by age twenty, the average players had logged about four thousand hours of practice time; the good violinists totaled about eight thousand hours; the elite performers set the standard with ten thousand hours.[2] While there is no denying that innate ability dictates some of your upside potential, your potential is only tapped via persistent effort. Persistence is the magic bullet, and the magic number seems to be around ten thousand.

Neurologist Daniel Levitin notes:

> The emerging picture from such studies is that ten thousand hours of practice is required to achieve the level of mastery associated with being a world-class expert — in anything. In study after study, of composers, basketball players, fiction writers, ice skaters, concert pianists, chess players, master criminals, and what have you, this number comes up again and again … No one has yet found a case in which true world-class expertise was accomplished in less time. It seems that it takes the brain this long to assimilate all that it needs to know to achieve true mastery.[3]

Is prayer any different?

It's a habit that you feed. It is a discipline to be developed. Prayer is a skill to be practiced. The more you pray, the more you learn to love it. Don't get me wrong; if you book ten thousand hours of pointless and directionless prayer, you won't get anywhere. To achieve mastery, it might take ten thousand hours of hard prayer. This I know for sure: the bigger your dream the harder you're going to have to pray.

A Small Cloud

There was another important drought in Israel several centuries before Honi made his mark in the sand. For three long years, there was no puddle jumping in Israel. Then the Lord promised Elijah that He would send rain, but like every good promise, Elijah still had to circle it with persistent prayer. So Elijah climbed to the top of Mount Carmel, fell on his face, and prayed for rain. Six times he told his servant to look toward the sea, but there was no sign of rain. Most of us would give up right around two or three times, right? We can't see any real difference with our natural eyes, so we stop praying. But when we do that, we allow our circumstances to get between God and us instead of putting God between us and our circumstances.

Like Honi who said, "I will not move from here," Elijah held his holy ground. He stood on the promise God had given him. I think Elijah would have prayed ten thousand times if that's what it took, but between the sixth and seventh prayer, there was a subtle shift in atmospheric pressure. After the seventh circle, Elijah's nearsighted servant strained his eyes and saw a small cloud the size of a man's hand rising from the sea.

What if Elijah had quit praying after the sixth circle? The miracle would have been forfeited, of course. But Elijah prayed through, and God came through. The sky turned black; heavy winds blew across the barren landscape; rain stirred up the dust for the first time in three years. And God is great with rain miracles. This wasn't just a light drizzle; it was a terrific rainstorm.[4]

It's easy to give up on dreams, miracles, and promises. We lose heart, lose patience, lose faith. Worst part is, it's like a slow leak; it happens without us even knowing, until our prayer life is completely flat.

A little while ago, I realized that I had stopped circling one of the seven miracles I had written on my prayer stone during the ten-day Pentecost fast I did years ago. I *had* believed that God would heal my asthma, but I got tired of asking. It felt like God had put me on hold, so I just hung up. Then a conversation with a friend reactivated my faith, and I've started circling that miracle again.

Is there some dream that God wants to resurrect? Is there some promise you need to reclaim? Is there some miracle you need to start believing for again?

The reason many of us give up too soon is that we feel like we've failed somehow if God doesn't answer our prayer. That isn't failure. The only way you can fail is if you stop praying.

I love that approach to prayer. I love that approach to life too! It's the circle maker's mantra: 100 percent of the prayers I don't pray won't get answered.

God's Grammar

There's an old preacher's sermon titled "God's Grammar." I've forgotten most of the sermons I've ever heard, and that's a little depressing as a preacher, but this one statement was unforgettable: "Never put a comma where God puts a period, and never put a period where God puts a comma."

Sometimes we see a period, but there's really just a comma. We think that God's silence is the end of the sentence, but it's just a break in His sentence. Praying through is the conjunction that allows God to not just finish the sentence, but to make a statement.

"Lord,... if you had been here, my brother would not have died. But I know that even now God will give you whatever you ask."[5]

Did you catch the conjunction? This is one of the most amazing statements of faith in the whole Bible, because of the little conjunction, *but*, right in the middle of Martha's announcement to Jesus. It seems like it should end after Martha says, "Lord, if you had been here, my brother would not have died." Why? Because her brother, Lazarus, has been dead for four days! It's old news. But Martha doesn't put a period there. She puts a comma. Even though her brother is dead and buried, she is still holding out hope.

The little phrase "even now" is underlined and circled in my Bible. Even when it seems like God is four days late, it's too soon to give up. So even when it might seem like your dream is dead and buried, it's too soon to put a period there. After all, *you can't never always sometimes tell.*

I'm putting Martha's faith into two categories here. First-degree faith says, "Lord, if you had been here, my brother would not have died." First-degree faith is preventative faith. Like Martha's prayer, she believed that Jesus could have kept her brother from dying. We ask God to keep bad things from happening all the time. So we pray for safety as we travel, or that our food won't make us sick on a mission trip, or that a half-hour of studying does the trick. And there's nothing wrong with that, but there is another dimension of faith that believes God can undo what has already been done. Second-degree faith is resurrection faith. It's a faith that refuses to put a period, accept disappointments, and just "live with it." It's a faith that believes it's not over until God says it's over. And it's illustrated by Martha's "even now" profession of faith: "But I know that even now God will give you whatever you ask."

So how do you go from first-degree faith to second-degree faith? Well, there is no easy answer. Hard times are the best teachers of hard prayer. Even when you feel like God's a million miles away or there seems to be more questions than answers, you put a comma. *Even then* you believe *even now.* And during those moments where God's grammar doesn't make sense, your persistence quotient will go through a major growth spurt.

Hyperlink

Let's go back to Elijah. Even after three years of drought and a nasty and longwinded bout with depression, Elijah believed that God could send rain *even now.*

I wonder if Israel's original rainmaker was Honi's childhood hero. And I wonder if Honi's persistence in prayer was linked to this miracle. *If God did it for Elijah, I'll bet He can do it for me.* And on that note, I can't help but wonder if Elijah's persistence in prayer was linked to the miracle of raining quail. *If God can send a quailstorm, I'm pretty sure He can send a thunderstorm.*

One thing's definite: our heaviest-duty prayers are linked to the promises of God. When you know you are praying the promises of God, you can pray with holy confidence. It's the difference between praying on thin ice and praying on solid ground. You don't have to second-guess yourself because you know that God wants you to double-click on His promises.

You might've heard your parents say, "God said it, I believe it, and that settles it." That's an old one! Here's a fresh take on that old truth: God said it, I've circled it, and that settles it.

It was settled on the cross when Jesus announced, "It is finished." It wasn't just the last episode of our sin saga; it began the new season of all His promises. "No matter how many promises God has made, they are 'Yes' in Christ."[6]

Time for a checkpoint. Remember the promise in Joshua 1:3 that I circled when I did my prayer walk around Capitol Hill? God promised Joshua that He would give him every place where he set his foot, but there is a little *P.S.* at the end of that promise: "as I promised Moses." The promise was originally given to Moses but Joshua inherited it. In the same way, all of God's promises have been transferred to us by Jesus Christ. What a deal! And it doesn't cost you anything — just faith. These promises should be interpreted intelligently and applied accurately; but there are moments when the Spirit of God will quicken your spirit to hang on to a promise that was originally intended for someone else, or get on board with something someone else is praying for. So while we have to be careful not to blindly claim promises that don't belong to us, our greatest challenge is that we don't always circle the promises we could or should circle.

There are somewhere around three thousand promises in Scripture. By virtue of what Jesus Christ accomplished on the cross, every one of them belongs to you. Every one of them has your name on it. The question is: How many of them have you circled?

Tree Island

Because this principle of linking our prayers to the promises of God is so important, let me paint another picture. The promises of God are the high ground, the holy ground, on which we stand. Circling those promises is the way we take our stand.

I have a friend who owns a log cabin on Lake Anna in central Virginia, and he has let me and my family vacation there a few times. During our first stay, my daughter Summer and I were six weeks out from the Escape from Alcatraz swim in San Francisco, so we put on wetsuits and did a training swim. There was a tree in the middle of the lake that looked like a good turnaround point. Plus, I'd never really seen anything quite like it, so we decided to swim out to it. Sure enough, it was literally a solitary tree that was growing on an island in the middle of the lake, and it was like five feet across. I have no idea how it got there, but you can actually see it on Google maps.

While we swam, Parker pulled my other son Josiah on an inner tube behind the pontoon boat. As we got closer to Tree Island, I told him to jump off the inner tube and swim over, but Josiah was afraid because we were in the middle of the lake. Like most eight-year-old kids, Josiah is a little more at home in the shallow end of a pool. What he didn't know is that the lake had gotten shallow as we approached Tree Island. I could feel it under my feet, but everybody else still thought it was deep because we were in the middle of the lake. So in one dramatic gesture, I literally stood up in the middle of the lake, and it looked like I was walking on water! When Josiah realized it wasn't all that deep, he jumped off the inner tube and swam over. Then *he* stood on water! For some reason, that's the mental image that comes to mind every time I think about standing on the promises of God.

The promises of God are like Tree Island in the middle of the lake. They are the difference between sinking and swimming, because they give you a place to stand, rest, and take it easy. And when God keeps His promises, you won't just stand on the water; you waltz into the Promised Land through the waters God has parted.

Start Circling

I'm going to share something I've learned over the years that I think could change the way you pray and read the Bible. We often view prayer and Scripture reading as two separate spiritual practices without much in common, but what if they were meant to be linked? What if reading became a form of praying and praying became a form of reading?

One of the biggest reasons we don't pray through is because we run out of things to say! Our lack of persistence is just a lack of conversation pieces. "Well. This is awkward ... Talk to you later, God!" And when that happens, our prayer turns into clichés and vague requests. Instead of praying hard about a big dream, we're left with small talk. Prayer becomes just about as fun as weather chat.

The solution? Pray through the Bible.

Prayer was never meant to be a one-sided conversation; it was meant to be a dialogue! Think of Scripture as God's part of the script; prayer's our part. Scripture is God's way of initiating a conversation, and prayer is just our response. The shift happens when you realize that the Bible wasn't just meant to be *read through*; the Bible was meant to be *prayed through*. And if you pray through it, you'll never run out of things to talk about.

The Bible is a promise book and a prayer book. And while reading is reactive, prayer is proactive. Reading is the way you just "get through" the Bible; prayer is the way you get the Bible through you. You think you've read it all? Not if you haven't prayed it. As you pray, the Holy Spirit will highlight certain promises to your spirit. It's very difficult to predict what and when and where and how, but over time, the promises of God will become *your* promises. Then you need to circle those promises, both figuratively and literally. I never read without my trusty pen so that I can mark my Bible up. As a result, my Bible is well worn and abused with circles and notes and stars and lines.

One of my most treasured possessions is my grandfather's Bible. Old Bibles are awesome! I love doing devotions in his Bible because I love seeing the verses he underlined and his notes in the margins. You know what else I love? You connected the dots — seeing the promises he circled. The best thing about his Bible is that it literally had to be taped together because it was falling apart. It wasn't just well read. It was well prayed.

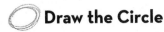 **Draw the Circle**

1. Where does persistence rate in your description of your prayer life? How would you grade your ability to push through and persist in prayer (praying when you don't feel like praying)? An A, B, C, D, or F? Why? (Keep in mind, the only way we can fail at prayer is when we stop praying!)

2. Have you ever put a period where God put a comma? Are there any prayers that you thought were a "no" but maybe they are a "not yet"?

3. List your favorite promises of God that you can recall from the Bible. (If you don't have any, or can't think of verses offhand, a youth pastor—or even a Bible reference guide—can help get you started.) The promises of God are key to praying with confidence and for even knowing what to say when we pray. Experiment with prayer by circling one of them for a week or a month.

Chapter 9

The Favor of Him Who Dwells
in the Burning Bush

The first time I saw the old crack house I was surprised such an eyesore existed just five blocks from the Capitol building. Cinder blocks filled the cavities where doors and windows once were. The brick walls were painted a snot-green color that must have come into and gone out of style very quickly many decades before. And the graffiti on the walls seemed like the appropriate finishing touch on our nuisance property.

I had walked by it at least a hundred times. In fact, I had walked right by the corner of 2nd and F Street NE when I prayed a circle around Capitol Hill fifteen years before. But as I walked by it this particular time, it was like the Holy Spirit put this dream in my heart: *This crack house would make a great coffeehouse.*

It was a crazy idea for so many reasons. First of all, no one on our staff had ever worked at a coffeehouse. Besides that, churches build *churches*, not coffeehouses. We had no business going into the coffeehouse business, but the more I thought about it the more it made sense in a nonsensical sort of way. After all, Jesus didn't just hang out at the synagogue. He hung out at wells, and wells were the hangout in ancient culture. One day it dawned on me that coffeehouses are the new wells. The only difference is that we draw shots of espresso instead of buckets of water.

So the dream of creating a "well" where our church and community could cross paths was born, and that dream is fulfilled hundreds of times every day with each customer who walks through our doors.

Ebenezer's Coffeehouse has been voted the #1 coffeehouse in the metro DC area.[1] The performance space doubles as one of our seven church campuses. To top it off, every penny of profit goes to local community projects and our humanitarian efforts in other countries. It's more than a miracle; it's a miracle squared.

You probably saw this coming. I'm going to retrace the circle once again.

Casing the Crack House

The coffeehouse really seemed like a crazy idea because NCC was just getting off the ground when the Holy Spirit gave us this God idea. We barely had any people or any money, but that's always the makings for great prayer. And we prayed hard for eight years! We laid hands on the walls and prayed. We knelt on the property and prayed. We fasted and prayed. And I lost count of how many circles we prayed around that old crack house.

I would usually pray around that property seven times a pop, going off the Jericho miracle. About lap five was when I would get strange looks from the security guards at the Federal Judiciary Building across the street. *Is this guy casing a crack house?* (Those guards are regular customers at our coffeehouse now!) And while I no longer circle the property in prayer, my favorite place to pray is the rooftop of Ebenezer's Coffeehouse. I climb the ladder, pop the hatch, and pray on the rooftop — so I'm still getting strange looks from the high-rise offices across the street. We've had more than one person ask why someone is pacing back and forth on the rooftop.

Where's your spot? Your favorite prayer place? The place where you can focus best or have a little more faith?

I love praying on top of the coffeehouse because I feel like I'm praying on top of a miracle. It's hard *not* to pray with faith when you're praying in a place where God has already done a miracle.

I bet that's how Elijah felt praying on Mount Carmel during Israel's drought. This was his home court, after all. God had just answered an impossible prayer right there. Elijah challenged the 450 prophets to a prayer duel on Mount Carmel as each side asked God to consume their sacrifice with fire. Elijah won that sudden-death showdown in dramatic fashion as God grilled his sacrifice.[2] The God who sent fire can obviously send rain, right? God's answer to Elijah gave him the faith he needed to pray hard. And that is one of the by-products of answered prayer. It gives us the faith to believe God for bigger and better miracles. With each answered prayer, we draw bigger prayer circles. With each act of faithfulness, our faith increases. With each promise kept, our persistence quotient grows.

Looking back, I'm glad the coffeehouse took eight years of hard prayer, because it stretched our faith in the process. When you have to pray that long, you aren't even tempted to take it for granted. This may sound commonsensical, but if it hadn't taken a miracle, it wouldn't be a miracle.

Binding Contract

Originally, the two lawyers who owned 201 F Street NE wanted $1 million for the crack house because of its location, location, location. It's just one block from Union Station and kitty-corner to the largest office building in DC, which is home to the Securities and Exchange Commission. The corner of 2nd and F Street NE also forms the NW corner of the Capitol Hill historic district.

We couldn't touch $1 million, so we prayed, and the harder we prayed the more the price dropped. We ultimately purchased the property for $325,000, but that was less of a miracle than the fact that four people offered more money for the property than we did. And two of them were real estate developers!

So how did we get it?

My only explanation is that we circled Matthew 18:18. Our prayers were linked to that promise, and we double-clicked it by praying hard.

"Whatever you bind on earth will be bound in heaven."[3]

The word *bind* means "to place a contract on something." This is precisely what happens when you pray. When you pray for something in the earthly realm, God puts a contract on it in the heavenly realm if you are praying in accordance with the will of God. So while February

7, 2002, is the date we signed the physical contract, the spiritual contract predates it by several years. The deal dates back to the first prayer circle we drew around it.

Watching and Waiting

The Bible tells us that the Lord is watching over His word to perform it.[4]

There is nothing God loves more than keeping His promises. He is actively watching and waiting for us to simply take Him at His word.[5] He's watching over each and every promise that He's made, and if that doesn't fill you with holy confidence, what will?

Praying hard is standing on the promises of God. And when we stand *on* His word, God stands *by* His word. His word is His bond.

How does the old song go? *I stand alone on the word of God, the B-I-B-L-E!* I bet you sang it in Sunday school.

We sometimes pray like God doesn't *want* to keep His promises, and we have to beg Him to. You have no idea how badly God wants to keep His promises! That's why He made them in the first place. We sometimes pray as if our bold prayers that circle the promises of God might offend the God who made them. Are you kidding me? God is offended by anything less! There's nothing God loves more than showing off His power. We only doubt God because we doubt *ourselves*. We don't ask God to extend His hand because we don't know His heart.

Psalm 84:11 captures the heart of the heavenly Father:

No good thing does he withhold
from those who walk uprightly.[6]

God isn't holding out or holding back at all. It's not in His nature to withhold any good thing from us. He won't bless disobedience, straight up, but He'll definitely bless obedience. If you take God at His word, it takes a load off your shoulders, because you realize He *wants* to bless you far more than you even want to be blessed. And His capacity to give is far greater than your capacity to receive.

I picked up a little quirk from my mom. No normal kid gets to open presents before a birthday or Christmas. Operative word: *nor-*

mal. That's not my family. My mom used to beg me to open my gifts before the appropriate day because she could hardly wait to give them! "Are you *sure*? Not even *one*? Here, just this small one! C'mon!" And now I do with our kids what she did with me. Parents begging their children to open their gifts early probably seems a little dysfunctional, but I think that's how the Heavenly Father feels about the art of gift giving. He can hardly wait to keep His promises. He can hardly wait to act on His word. He can hardly wait to answer our prayers. And when we just take Him at His word, He can hardly contain His joy. True story.

My favorite sentence in the twenty-third psalm is this: "Surely goodness and mercy shall follow me all the days of my life."[7] The word *follow* isn't even a strong enough translation. It's a hunting term in Hebrew. This is awesome: it's like God is literally tracking and hunting you down — but not to harm you. God is hunting you down to bless you. He wants to show us His goodness and His mercy, but too often we run away from it. Why? Because we doubt His good intentions. We can't believe that God is for us. *It's too good to be true.* But it's entirely true.

The Favor of Him Who Dwelt in the Burning Bush

If you asked me what I pray for more than anything else, the answer is the favor of God. It's tough to describe or define, but I think the favor of God is what God does for you that you can't do for yourself. I pray the favor of God around NCC. I pray the favor of God around the books I write, my family, and countless other things. The favor of God is divine insurance!

The longer I live, the more I crave the favor of God. The greatest moments in life are those moments when God steps in and blesses us way beyond what we expect or deserve. It's a humble reminder of His sovereignty. And these favor moments become our favor-ite memories. (The puns keep coming!)

I'll never forget August 12, 2001.

National Community was a fledgling church for five years. If you grew up on a farm, you'll get this analogy. Planting a church in DC is like plowing rock-hard soil. Better yet, it's like milking a chicken (I won't go into detail). It took us five years to grow from our core group of 19 to 250 people. Then it was almost like the Lord declared, "Now is the time of God's favor."[8]

A religion reporter from *The Washington Post* asked for an interview because she was intrigued by how surprisingly young our congregation was. She proceeded to write an article about how we were reaching younger generations and told me that I'd see it in the religion section. I made sure to pick up a two-inch-thick Sunday edition on my way into Union Station that morning and quickly flipped to the religion section. I was bummed when I didn't find the article. I figured it didn't make the editorial cut, so I put the newspaper back on the stand because I wasn't going to buy it if we weren't in it. That's when I discovered that the article was on the front page!

That was the day God put NCC on the map. It had taken five years to grow to 250 people, but we doubled in size over the next year. It was as though God had opened the floodgates of favor, and hundreds of readers visited National Community Church as a result of that one article. And the beautiful thing about it is that we couldn't take credit for it. It was nothing more, or maybe I should say nothing less, than the favor of God. It was God's time. It was God's favor. It was God's word. And God was watching over it.

Every verse on favor is circled in my Bible, but my personal favorite is one of the blessings that Moses pronounced over Joseph:

May the Lord bless his land
with the precious dew from heaven above
and with the deep waters that lie below;
with the best the sun brings forth
and the finest the moon can yield;
with the choicest gifts of the ancient mountains
and the fruitfulness of the everlasting hills;
with the best gifts of the earth and its fullness
and the favor of him who dwelt in the burning bush.[9]

Did you catch "the favor" in the last phrase? God's favor is multidimensional, but this might rank as my favorite kind: "the favor of him who dwelt in the burning bush." And I love the fact that this blessing is pronounced by Moses himself. He knew what he was describing because he was the one who heard the Voice in the bush.

The hard thing about praying hard is letting God do the heavy lifting. You have to trust the favor of God to do for you what you cannot do for yourself. You have to trust God to change hearts, even if it's one as hard as the heart of Pharaoh.

Full Circle

Since we're pretty much in full-blown circle mode at this point, let me circle all the way back to the old crack house.

We prayed for that old crack house at 201 F Street NE for several years before I finally mustered up the courage to call the phone number listed on the For Sale sign. I felt foolish. What was I going to say? "Hi, I'm the pastor of a church with no people and no money. We'd like to buy your crack house and turn it into a coffeehouse." It sounded so beyond ridiculous, and I thought it would sound even more ridiculous to them. But, believe it or not, that's precisely what God told me to say. So I said it.

I knew that the two lawyers who owned the property, both of whom were Jewish, might not understand or appreciate who we were or what we wanted to do as a church, but I felt like God wanted me to humbly yet boldly tell them who we were and what we wanted to do. So I didn't pull any punches. I prayed for favor. Then I shared our vision like I was casting it to our congregation. And guess what? They loved it. My only explanation for their reaction is the favor of Him who dwells in the burning bush.

The favor of Him who dwells in the burning bush is a unique dimension of God's favor that enables you to stand before those who would naturally stand in opposition to you, but they supernaturally step aside or stand behind you. That's how the favor of Him who dwells in the burning bush expressed itself when Moses stood before Pharaoh. It gave a slave (and, mind you, there's a warrant out for his arrest) the boldness to declare the promise God had given him at the burning bush: "Let my people go."[10]

Purchasing the property at 2nd and F Street was the first miracle in the process of building Ebenezer's Coffeehouse. I would not recommend this kind of risk unless you know it is Spirit prompted, but we purchased the property knowing that we would need to get a change in the zoning code in order to build the coffeehouse. If our rezoning efforts were unsuccessful, our dream would die. I'll cut to the chase. It took eighteen months, $3 million, and a ton of patience! Some crazy neighbors decided to squash our rezoning effort and I got ticked off. Their opposition had the potential to short-circuit the whole operation and God's plan, and I got angrier and angrier every time I thought about it. That's when I discovered the power of praying circles around the pharaohs in your life. Every time I got angry, I converted that anger into a prayer. Let's just say that I came as close as I had ever come to praying without ceasing!

I prayed for those neighbors for several months leading up to our hearing before the zoning commission. I'll never forget the feeling as we walked into the hearing room and sat down at our tables on either side of the aisle. I wouldn't have thought it would be the case originally, but I just didn't feel any bitterness toward them. I felt compassion for the people who opposed us, and I wasn't worried at all about what they said or did because I had circled them in prayer. I had also circled the zoning commissioners. Not only did we win unanimous approval from the Zoning Commission, which is a testament to the favor of Him who dwells in the burning bush, but one of those people who opposed us is now a regular customer at Ebenezer's.

I'm sure this seems irrelevant to your life, all these property miracles. You're in high school, maybe college, and I'm telling you about *real estate*. Understandable. But look past the content and ask, who are the pharaohs in your life? Circle them in prayer. It'll make you a cool, calm person, which will become very important in the adult world. You're in a fight with your girlfriend. Pray for favor in her life. Your teacher's giving you endless detentions (my kids have been there); pray for peace in their life. It applies to everything, not just real estate.

I'm not going to lie. The entire two-year ordeal of rezoning was emotionally and spiritually exhausting, but that's how you increase your persistence quotient. It taught us how to pray like it depends on God and work like it depends on us. It only reassured me that we don't have to be afraid of the enemy's attacks. They're counterproductive when we counteract them with prayer. The more opposition we experience, the harder we have to pray, and the harder we have to pray, the more miracles God does.

Draw the Circle

1. When has God blessed you far beyond what you expected or thought you deserved?

2. There is nothing God wants to do more than prove His power by keeping His promises. Do you pray that way? What difference does this make in our attitude, expectation, and tenacity in prayer? Have you ever noticed that difference?

3. Is it difficult for you to believe God wants good things for you? Is it difficult for you to receive such blessings? Why? How has this held you back in your prayer life? Read Psalm 84:11 and remind yourself of the heart of your Heavenly Father!

Chapter 10

Game of Chicken

Remember the game Chicken? From first grade? God must love the game of Chicken because He plays it with us all the time. He has this habit of waiting until the very last moment to answer our prayer to see if we'll *chicken out* or *pray through*. If we chicken out, we miss out on the miracle; if we pray through, God will come through, but it may well be at the last moment possible. And, of course, if you chicken out of the game of Chicken, God will always give you another chance to get back in the game and play another round.

The classic last-second provision is repeated throughout Scripture, and I think it reveals God's playful personality. Sometimes we're so focused on the character of God that we forget that God has a personality too. He loves hiding around corners and jumping out and scaring the mess out of us with blessings. You can't convince me that Jesus didn't have fun sneaking up on the disciples in the middle of the night in the middle of the lake by walking on water. I can just imagine them waking up everyone around the lake with girly cries of "Help! It's a ghost!" There's no way God didn't enjoy the befuddled look on Moses's face when he heard the talking bush. Probably why He chose a bush! As I read Scripture, I can come to no other conclusion than this: God loves showing up in unexpected ways at unexpected times.

I love this part of God's personality. In big and small ways, it's prayer that adds the unexpected twists and turns in our personal plotlines that make life so worth living. It's prayer that can turn any story, your story, into an epic drama.

I have scribbled the initials *JEJIT* in the margins of my Bible at various places where God provides *just enough just in time*. He did it with the widow who is down to her last jar of olive oil.[1] He did it when the Israelites are trapped between the Egyptian army and Red Sea.[2] He did it when the boat is about to capsize on the Sea of Galilee because of hurricane-force winds.[3] And He's done it for us countless times when it seemed we were involved in a cosmic game of Chicken with God.

Maybe you're in a desperate situation right now. That means one thing: God is setting the stage for a miracle. I know for sure that God is always stage right. He's ready to make His grand entrance. All He's waiting for is your prayer cue.

The Manna Miracle

When God provided the miraculous manna for the Israelites as they wandered in the wilderness, it says He provided "enough for that day."[4] *Just enough*. The description's pretty precise. Those who gathered a lot had nothing left over, and those who gathered a little had enough. God provided just enough. Then He gave them a curious command: "Do not keep any of it until morning."[5]

So why does God provide just enough? Why would God forbid leftovers? What's wrong with taking a little initiative and gathering enough manna for a couple days or weeks?

Here's my take on the manna miracle: The manna was a daily reminder of their daily dependence on God. God wanted to cultivate their daily dependence by providing for their needs on a daily basis. Nothing's changed. Isn't that the point of the Lord's Prayer? "Give us today our daily bread."[6]

We want a one-week or one-month or one-year supply of God's provision, but God wants us to drop to our knees every day in raw dependence on Him. And God knows that if He provided too much too soon, we'd lose our spiritual hunger. He knows we'd stop trusting in our Provider and start trusting in the provision.

Spiritual maturity is often confused with independence. It's the exact opposite. The goal is codependence on God. I understand the desire to grow into adulthood, do your own thing, move out of the house, live your own life away from your parents, but God didn't design us to "grow up" and be independent from Him. Our desire for self-sufficiency is a subtle expression of our sinful nature. It's a desire to get to a place where we don't need God, don't need faith, don't need a local church home, and don't need to pray. We want God to provide more so we need Him less. That's just not the way it's supposed to work.

Holy Complications

One reason many people get frustrated spiritually is that they feel like it should get easier to do the will of God. I don't know if this will be encouraging or disheartening, but the will of God doesn't get any easier. The will of God gets harder. Here's why: the harder it gets, the harder you have to pray.

God will keep putting you in situations that stretch your faith, and as your faith stretches, so do your dreams. What happens when you pass a test? You graduate to bigger and bigger things and dreams. And it won't get easier; it'll get harder. It won't get less complicated; it'll get more complicated. But complications are evidence of God's blessing. And if it's from God, then it's a holy complication. Nothing wrong with that.

You need to come to terms with this two-sided truth: The blessings of God won't just bless you; they'll also complicate your life. Sin will complicate your life in negative ways. The blessings of God will complicate your life in positive ways. When I married Lora, it complicated my life, and it *really* complicated her life! Praise God for complications. We have three complications named Parker, Summer, and Josiah. I can't imagine my life without those complications. As you move into higher education, your classes will become more complicated. With every promotion, there are complications. My point? Blessings will complicate your life, but they will complicate your life in ways God wants it complicated.

A few years ago, I prayed a prayer that changed my life. I believe it can change your life as well, but it takes tremendous courage to pray it like you mean it. And you have to count the cost.

Lord, complicate my life.

Afflict the Comfortable

Let's be honest: many, if not most, of our prayers are more selfish than we care to admit. We pray as if God's chief objective is our personal comfort. It's not. God's chief objective is His glory. And sometimes His gain involves a little pain.

Sometimes we pray without considering the consequences. When I pray that God will bless National Community Church, I'm praying that God will make my life more complicated and less comfortable. It was much more comfortable when the church had twenty-five people. It was much less complicated when we had one service at one location. As God has blessed NCC, I've had to count the cost. On a very practical level, the answer to my prayers meant giving up more of my weekend to God. When we launched a Saturday night and Sunday night service, the cost was two more time slots every weekend that I gave back to God. Here's the bottom line: Praying hard is asking God to make your life harder. The harder you pray, the harder you will have to work. Look at it this way: your life was going to get harder and more complicated anyway. You can get into sin complications or God complications — your choice. The difference is that you're reimbursed for having God complicate your life. Sin is another story.

You can't just be willing to pray about something; you also have to be willing to do a thing or two about it. And this is where many of us get stuck spiritually. We're willing to pray right up to the point of discomfort, but no further. We're willing to pray right up to the point of inconvenience, but no more after that. Praying hard is uncomfortable and inconvenient, but that's when you know you're getting close to a miracle!

The reason God doesn't answer our prayers isn't that we aren't praying hard enough; the reason, more often than not, is that we aren't willing to work hard enough. Praying hard should be the same as working hard. Think of praying hard and working hard as concentric circles. It's the way we double-circle our dreams and His promises. There comes a moment, after you have prayed through, when you have to start doing something about it. You have to take a step of faith, and that first step is always the hardest.

Woolly Socks

I recently spoke at Church of the Highlands in Birmingham, Alabama, for my friend Chris Hodges. I toured their Dream Center in downtown Birmingham because we want to do something similar in DC. They have an amazing outreach to pimps and prostitutes. They mentor kids. They feed the hungry. You name the need, and they're meeting it.

A woman there named Lisa likes to play Chicken with God. She's one of those people who overflows with joy, life, and energy. She left her job to serve the poor, broken, and hungry at the Dream Center and she daily sees God come through at the last moment.

During our tour, Lisa talked about their daily dependence on God to meet the overwhelming needs in their community. It takes hard work and hard prayer. Then she told me about one of the miracles she had experienced. One day, as she was circling the Dream Center in prayer, she heard one of those Holy Spirit whispers and felt like she should take her woolly socks with her to work. It was one of the strangest promptings she'd ever had, and she thought she was losing her mind, but she couldn't shake the impression. So she grabbed her wool socks, put them in her purse, and headed downtown. When she got there, a prostitute was literally passed out on the doorstep. Lisa opened the door, carried her inside, and cradled her in her arms until she came to a few minutes later. The woman was so cold that she was shaking. That's when Lisa asked her, "If you could have anything, what would it be?" Without hesitation, she said, "Wool socks." Lisa about lost it. As she told me the story, she started tearing up. Then I started tearing up! Lisa told her, "Look what I have." She pulled out the woolly socks, and the young woman said, "They even match my outfit."

God is great not just because nothing is too big for Him; God is great because nothing is too small for Him. A sparrow doesn't fall without His noticing and caring, so it shouldn't surprise us that He cares about a woman who wants woolly socks. God loves showing His all-encompassing compassion in little ways, and if we would learn to obey His nudging and whispers like Lisa, we might just find ourselves in the middle of miracles more often.

The reason we sometimes miss miracles is because we aren't looking or listening for them. The easy part of prayer is talking. It's much harder listening to the still, small voice of the Holy Spirit. It's much harder looking for the answers. But two-thirds of praying hard is listening and looking.

Wet Feet

When the Israelites were on the verge of entering the Promised Land, God commanded the priests to not just look toward the sea but to step into the river. It's one of the most illogical commands in Scripture.

"When you reach the banks of the Jordan River, take a few steps into the river."[7]

I don't know about you, but I don't really like getting my feet wet all that much. I'd much rather have God part the river, and *then* I'll step into the miracle. We want God to go first. That way we don't have to get our feet wet. But it's often our unwillingness to take a step of faith and get a little uncomfortable that keeps us from experiencing a miracle. We'll spend our entire lives on the eastern shore of the Jordan waiting for God to part the river while God waits for us to get our feet wet. After you have prayed hard, you need to swallow hard and take a flying leap of faith. That's how you circle the miracle.

At flood tide, the Jordan River was about a mile wide. That was all that separated the Israelites from their four-hundred-year-old promise. One mile! Their dream was a stone's throw away. But what if the priests hadn't stepped into the river? What if they had sat around waiting for God to do His parting thing? Sometimes we're so close to the dream, so close to the promise, so close to the miracle, but unless we risk stepping forward, we get stuck. We end up living our entire lives on the eastern banks of the Jordan River instead of crossing into the Promised Land.

Moral of the story: if you make a move, you'll see God move. And He can move heaven and earth.

Prayer Promptings

Peter's got to be the patron saint of wet feet. He may have failed the persistence test, but he passed the wet-feet test by getting out of a boat in the middle of the Sea of Galilee when Jesus called out one of the craziest commands in Scripture: "Come."[8] Peter risked far more than wet feet. The Sea of Galilee was a 91-square-mile dunk tank, and he was in the middle of it in the middle of the night.

The key to getting out of the boat is hearing the voice of God. If you're going to get out of the boat in the middle of a lake in the middle of the night, you better make sure that Jesus said, "Come." But if Jesus *does* say, "Come," I highly suggest getting out of that boat!

Have you ever had a Lisa-moment when the Holy Spirit prompted you during prayer to do something that seemed borderline crazy? Have you ever had a Peter-moment when God called you to do something that seemed unsafe? Your response to those promptings will make you or break you. It may seem unsafe or insane, but if you stay in the boat, you won't be walking on any water.

A few years ago, a friend of mine shared one of his prayer promptings with me because, little did I know, it involved me. I was on a speaking trip, away from my family, when God woke Rick up in the middle of the night. He felt the Lord prompting him to pray for my family, and the prompting was *so* intense that he woke up his roommates. (I bet he asked God to confirm it was really necessary to wake them up!) After praying, Rick felt like they needed to drive over to our house. So at four in the morning they trucked across the Hill, parked in front of our place, and prayed for my family. He said to me afterward, "This has never happened to me before. I don't know why God got me up at four in the morning, but we knew we needed to pray for you."

I honestly have no idea why God prompted him to pray that way, but some of God's greatest answers to prayer won't be revealed on this side of eternity because they're invisible answers. When God makes something happen, we can thank Him because we can see it. When God keeps something from happening, we don't know how to thank Him because we don't know what He did. But I can't wait for God to show me what was *really* going on that night that He prevented from happening.

A lot of people, especially teenagers, ask, "Why don't I hear that distinct voice of God?" Well, I've found that it's impossible to hear His mighty voice without listening to and obeying the small voice of His spirit. And picking up on that voice takes time, and faith.

Go Fish

Let me paint one more picture. It only seems appropriate, since praying is a lot like fishing. More than anything else, it involves a lot of patience.

> *After Jesus and his disciples arrived in Capernaum, the collectors of the two-drachma temple tax came to Peter and asked, "Doesn't your teacher pay the temple tax?"*
>
> *"Yes, he does," he replied.*
>
> *When Peter came into the house, Jesus was the first to speak. "What do you think, Simon?" he asked. "From whom do the kings of the earth collect duty and taxes — from their own children or from others?"*
>
> *"From others," Peter answered.*
>
> *"Then the children are exempt," Jesus said to him. "But so that we may not cause offense, go to the lake and throw out your line. Take the first fish you catch; open its mouth and you will find a four-drachma coin. Take it and give it to them for my tax and yours."[9]*

This has to rank as one of the wildest commands in Scripture. Part of me wonders if Peter thought Jesus was joking. He was probably a little off-balance, because I'm sure Jesus had pulled more than one prank on Peter.

So why does Jesus do it this way? He could have provided the four-drachma coin in the normal way by giving it to him, but He tells Peter to go fish for it. I think there are a few reasons. First of all, God loves doing different miracles in different ways because it reveals different dimensions of His power and personality. But I wonder if the biggest reason is that Jesus wanted to see if Peter would trust Him in the realm where Peter had the greatest professional expertise. As a professional fisherman, fishing was the one area where Peter would have been most tempted to think he didn't need Jesus. He thought he knew every trick of the fishing trade, but Jesus wanted to show him a new trick. We'll call it "the coin in the mouth of the fish" trick.

We know how the story ends. Peter catches a fish and cashes in a nasty coin. But if you've caught hundreds of thousands of fish, none of which has ever had a coin in its mouth, how do you have the faith to believe that the next one will have a four-drachma coin? It seems kind of impossible, doesn't it? But there's only one way to find out if God will keep His promise: Obey the crazy nudges.

Now let's take it a step further: Where do you feel like you need God least? Where are you most talented and gifted, most adequate? Maybe that is precisely where God wants you to trust Him to do something *beyond* your ability. That's *not* all folks, because it's just when you think you have God all figured out that He pulls the coin out of the fish's mouth. And it's God's strange and mysterious ways that renew our awe, our trust, and our dependence.

Let me spell it out: If you want to see crazy miracles, obey the crazy promptings of the Holy Spirit. Grab your pole, head to the lake, row the boat, cast the line, set the hook, and reel it in. As you obey the promptings by casting your line, you never know what you'll catch, but you can expect miracles.

Go fish.

Draw the Circle

1. Have you chickened out when God called you to do something? How? What did you learn from it?

2. Think of the JEJIT concept — *just enough just in time*. Recall a time in your life when God came through with just enough just in time. Why do you think God sometimes waits until the very last minute to come through? Why do you think He sometimes provides just what is needed at the moment and not a bit more?

3. God is great not just because nothing is too big for Him; God is great because nothing is too small for Him. How does this picture of God's all-encompassing compassion make you feel? What have you not brought to Him in prayer because you considered it too small for His attention?

Chapter 11

No Answer

For a big chunk of my life, basketball *was* my life. When I graduated from high school, I went to the University of Chicago on a full-ride scholarship and earned a starting position on the basketball team by the end of my freshman year. Then I transferred to Central Bible College, where I earned first-team all-American honors my senior season. Of course, it was the NCCAA, not the NCAA; the extra C stands for Christian. I was our leading scorer, averaging 21.3 points per game, and we were favorites to win the national championship, the NCCAA championship.

I was having my best season ever, and I wasn't just playing well; I was playing for God. I wanted to win a national championship because I thought it would be a great way to glorify God, but that dream died with one cut to the basket when my right knee buckled. Two weeks before the national tournament, my basketball career came to a painful end with a torn anterior cruciate ligament (an injury no athlete ever wants to deal with).

To be honest, the spiritual pain was worse than the physical pain. At first, I was angry. *God, I was playing for you. How could you let this happen?* Eventually, my anger turned to mourning, and then my mourning turned to begging. I remember weeping in prayer and begging God to heal my knee. I knew He could do it, but for reasons unknown to me, He chose not to. I was demoted to cheering for my teammates as we lost in the semifinals. In the grand scheme of things, I realize that a game is a game, but it was a bitter disappointment. And I still don't know why.

Some of the hardest moments in life are when you actually *do* pray hard but the answer is no and you don't know why. And you may never know why, but it's part of the trust test. Do you trust that God is for you even when He doesn't give you what you asked for? Do you trust that He has reasons beyond your reason? Do you trust that His plan is better than yours?

There are some mysteries that won't be revealed until we cross into eternity. I don't understand why God wouldn't heal my knee. I don't understand why my father-in-law passed away in the prime of life. I don't understand why loved ones have lost babies or gotten divorced. I have a lot of unanswered questions, and many of them derive from unanswered prayers.

The hardest thing about praying hard is enduring unanswered prayers. If you don't guard your heart, unresolved anger toward God can undermine faith. Sometimes your only option is trust because it is the last card in your hand, but it's the wild card. If you can trust God when the answer is no, you're likely to give Him praise when the answer is yes. You need to press in and press on. By definition, praying hard is praying when it's hard to pray. And it's the hard times that teach us to pray hard. But if you keep praying through, the peace that goes beyond understanding will guard your heart and your mind.

So sometimes the answer to our prayers is a straight up no and you'll never understand why. But here's some good news: What we perceive as unanswered prayers are often the greatest answers.

What's Going On?

During our first two years of church planting, our church office was in the spare bedroom in our home. It was a convenient commute, but it eventually became a huge inconvenience when our daughter, Summer, was born. Our spare bedroom turned into her bedroom by night and my office by day. I would set up her porta-crib at night and tear it down in the morning. That got real old real fast, so we started looking for office space.

After a few months of searching, I finally found a row house in the 400 block of F Street NE that we could convert into offices. It was perfectly situated halfway between our home and Union Station, and it had the ideal floor plan. We prayed that God would give us that contract, but when we presented the offer the next morning, we discovered that someone beat us to the punch the night before. It felt like a sucker punch that knocks the wind out of you. I was sure that this row house was the answer we were looking for, so it was both confusing and frustrating.

It took a few days to recuperate from that disappointment, but we resumed our search. A few weeks later, we found a row home in the 600 block of 3rd Street NE, just two blocks from Union Station. It was even more perfect than the previous place, so we prayed even harder. Once again, when we presented the offer the next morning, we discovered that someone got in ahead of us the night before. It felt like a second sucker punch to my faith.

After two bitter setbacks, I threw my arms up in the air. It was one of those "What's going on, God?" moments. Not only was God not answering our prayers; it felt like He was opposing our efforts. It felt like God was actually getting in the way. And He was. Good thing too!

The Greatest Answers

Two weeks later, after those two unanswered prayers, I was walking home from Union Station. As I passed by 205 F Street, the Holy Spirit jogged my memory, and a name surfaced out of the deep recesses of my long-term memory. I had met the owner a year before, but I'm not very good with names, so it's a miracle that I remembered *Robert Thomas* out of nowhere. And I felt prompted to call him.

There was no For Sale sign on the property, but I knew I needed to obey that prayer nudge, so I looked up his name in the Yellow Pages and found several listings for Robert Thomas. I made an educated guess and dialed the number. When he answered, I said, "Hi, this is Mark Batterson. I don't know if you remember me, but — " He didn't even let me finish my sentence. He interrupted me with, "I was just thinking about you. I'm thinking about selling 205 F Street, and I wanted to know if you want to buy it before I put it on the market."

Only God.

That row home became our first office, but even more significant than its function was its location. 205 F Street connects to 201 F Street. We started laying hands on those neighboring walls and asking God to give us the old crack house next door. I refused to believe that it was coincidental. I chose to believe it was providential. And it was.

If God had answered our prayers for the row homes in the 400 Block of F or 600 Block of 3rd, He would have given us second or third best. I was frustrated and confused because they seemed like good options, but they weren't the *best* option. And God doesn't settle for what's *good enough*. In His providence, God knew that we needed 205 F Street if we were going to eventually get 201 F Street. Because of construction and zoning complications, it would have been impossible for us to build our coffeehouse at 201 F if we hadn't owned 205 F.

Thank God for unanswered prayers!

Our heavenly Father is far too wise and loves us far too much to give us everything we ask for. Someday we'll thank God for the prayers He didn't answer as much or more than the ones He did. Our frustration will turn to celebration if we patiently and persistently pray through. It may not make sense for a few years. In fact, it may never make sense on this side of eternity. But I've learned a valuable lesson about unanswered prayer: *Sometimes God gets in the way to show us the way.*

Talking Donkeys

One of the wackiest miracles in the Bible involves a talking donkey. A prophet named Balaam is headed to Moab because he's been offered a nice sum of money to curse the Israelites. On his way, an angel of the Lord gets in the way. Balaam doesn't see the angel, but his donkey does. Three times the donkey saves Balaam's life by stopping, but Balaam is infuriated at his dumb donkey. That's when God opens the donkey's mouth, and it says to Balaam, "What have I done to you to make you beat me these three times?"[1] Remember, the donkey saved him three times. Balaam's response? "You have made a fool of me! If only I had a sword in my hand, I would kill you right now."

In all fairness, I don't think any one of us knows how we would respond if one of our pets just started talking to us! But Balaam is so enraged that he's not thinking straight. Dude, if you have a talking donkey on your hands, the last thing you want to do is kill it! You don't even need that chunk of change anymore! You're going to make a fortune. You can take your talking donkey show on the road. Go to Vegas.

I love the donkey's rational response. And I can't help but wonder if he had a distinguished British accent to go along with his superior intellect. "Am I not your own donkey, which you have always ridden, to this day? Have I been in the habit of doing this to you?"

The most respected prophet in the ancient world has zero comebacks. His only response to his cultured donkey is, "No." And he probably mumbled it.

Then the Lord opened Balaam's eyes to see the angel of the Lord, who said this to Balaam:

> *"I have come here to oppose you because your path is a reckless one before me. The donkey saw me and turned away from me these three times. If it had not turned away, I would certainly have killed you by now, but I would have spared it."[2]*

Sometimes we get ticked off Balaam-style when we can't get to where we want to go. We hate detours! They're frustrating. They are confusing. But the divine detours often get us where God wants us to go. The real miracle in this story isn't the talking donkey; the real miracle is a God who loves us enough to get in the way when we're going the wrong way. These are the miracles we don't really prefer, but they *are* the miracles we need. And when I look back on my own life, I'm grateful for the moments God got in the way of my plans and rerouted me. What seems like an unanswered prayer means that God has a better answer.

When I was a senior in college, I was offered a staff position with one of my heroes in ministry. He was a charismatic leader and awesome speaker. It felt like a dream job, but as I paced our chapel balcony praying about it, I felt a check in my spirit. It felt like God was getting in the way. I knew I needed to say no, but I didn't know why. I turned down the offer and went to graduate school instead. Less than a year later, this pastor had an affair, left his family and his church, and eventually committed suicide. I have no doubt that God could have protected me in that situation, but he kept me from it altogether. He rerouted me from Missouri to Illinois.

Then, while I was in seminary in the Chicago area, I tried to start a new church, but once again it felt like God got in the way. It was the wrong time and the wrong place. As you know, that new church imploded, and God rerouted us from Illinois to Washington, DC. And I'm so glad He did. I wouldn't want to be anyplace else doing anything else with anyone else. Our destiny was in DC, but God had to get in the way a few times to get us there. He had to leave a few prayers unanswered so that He could give a better answer.

To you, I'm sure it seems like I have it figured out because I talk about destiny and direction. But let's be honest, I'm telling these stories years down the road. It makes sense in hindsight. In the moment I was scared like anyone else would be. And you're still in the beginning of your life, so it's hard for you to look back and see prayers that God answered because you probably weren't on the top of your prayer game when you were *ten*. And I don't have it all figured out, just to reassure you. I simply know you have to pray hard now so you *can* look back and praise God for his miraculous answers.

I'm so grateful that God doesn't answer all of my prayers. He just has a better plan.

The Red Carpet

Fire code violations. Ever heard of them? I hate them! We were on the verge of becoming a homeless church because we received notice that the public school where we met was shutting down because of fire code violations. We had nowhere to go. We looked into at least twenty-five options, but every door we knocked on was slammed in our face. That's when I dared to dream big and pray hard. And while I've already shared the story of approaching the manager of the movie theaters at Union Station, here's the rest of the story.

Before asking the manager if we could rent the movie theaters on

Sunday mornings, I prayed seven circles around Union Station. It was no easy task weaving through commuters, taxicabs, and tourist buses. Actually, I prayed seven circles around Union Station on several occasions. Need courage? Pray lots of circles. Finally, after circling Union Station long enough to build up enough courage, I walked in the front doors, through the Great Hall, down the escalator, under the marquee, and into the theater.

It felt like God was shutting us down again, but he was just setting us up. Three days before I walked into the theater, AMC Theatres rolled out a nationwide program recruiting businesses and nonprofits to use their theaters when the screens were dark. As far as I know, we were the first group to respond to that initiative, and we had no idea it was going on! But God did. And God didn't just open an amazing door of opportunity; He rolled out the red carpet.

On the way out of Union Station, after signing a lease with the theater, I picked up *A History of Washington's Grand Terminal*. I immediately opened it, and the first thing I saw was an italicized phrase on the first page: "and for other purposes."

That phrase was part of the Bill of Congress signed by Teddy Roosevelt on February 28, 1903. It stated simply, "A Bill of Congress to create a Union Station and for other purposes." It's that last phrase, *and for other purposes*, that jumped off the page and into my spirit. Nearly a hundred years after that bill passed, Union Station started serving *God's purposes* through the ministry of NCC. Roosevelt thought he was building a train station. He had no idea that he was building a church — a church with a mass transportation system, parking garage, and forty-restaurant food court, no less! And our church was funded by Congress!

As I look back, I laugh at the fact that we were so scared when the doors to Giddings School closed. If God hadn't closed those doors, we would have never looked for the open door at Union Station. And that's the way it works: God closes doors in order to open bigger and better doors.

One of my most circled promises is Revelation 3:7 – 8. I've circled it hundreds of times in hundreds of different ways.

What he opens no one can shut, and what he shuts no one can open.... See, I have placed before you an open door that no one can shut.

In recent years, I've realized that I only circled half of that promise. I prayed for open doors but not closed doors. Quite frankly, we love it when God opens doors for us! When God slams a door in our face? Not so much! But you can't half-circle the promise. It's a package deal. You can't pray for open doors if you aren't willing to accept closed doors, because one leads to the other.

Stand Still

Thirteen years after walking through the open doors at Union Station, those doors were slammed shut. On a Monday morning in October 2009, I got a phone call from the theater manager at Union Station informing me that Union Station management was shutting down the theaters. She told me that the next Sunday would be our last Sunday. We didn't even have time to be sad because we had six days to figure out how to share the news with our congregation. My mind was on spin cycle.

Part of the reason the phone call was so devastating is that we had prayed hard that God would miraculously help us buy those movie theaters. Instead, we lost the lease. That hurts! Even though this had happened before, and we knew God would provide, it still felt like an anti-miracle. We had no idea where to go or what to do, but that's when God has us right where He wants us.

That week, our entire team was scheduled to attend the Catalyst Conference in Atlanta, Georgia. I was tempted to cancel the trip to keep working on an emergency evacuation plan for Union Station. It seemed like terrible timing, but it was perfect timing. Sometimes you have to get out of your routine so God can speak to you in a non-routine way. I knew that I couldn't just preach a sermon that weekend; I needed a word from the Lord. And God gave me one. During one of the teaching sessions at the conference, God gave me a promise to stand on and I put every ounce of my weight on Exodus 14:13 – 14:

"Don't be afraid. Just stand still and watch the LORD rescue you today. The Egyptians you see today will never be seen again. The LORD himself will fight for you. Just stay calm."³

What would be the hardest thing to do with the Egyptian army charging straight at you at full speed? The hardest thing to do is precisely what God told them to do: *stand still.* God doesn't just play Chicken; He also plays flinch. When we find ourselves in this kind of situation, we want to do something. Anything! We have a nervous energy that wants to solve the problem as quickly as possible. But God tells them to do nothing but pray. The closer the Egyptian army got, the more intense their prayers became. They clenched their jaws. They stood their holy ground. They prayed like they'd never prayed before.

Just in Time

All of us love miracles. We just don't like being in a situation that demands one. We hate finding ourselves between an Egyptian army and a Red Sea, but that's how God reveals His glory. We want God to part the Red Sea when the Egyptian army is still in Egypt. We want God to provide for our need before we even need it. But sometimes God waits. And then He waits longer. At first, the Israelites can see a dust cloud in the distance. Then they can hear the hooves of their horses and the wheels on their chariots. Then they're so close that they can recognize the faces of their former taskmasters ready to kill them for escaping.

This is intense! Put yourself in their shoes. The Israelites are sitting ducks, and God is the one who led them to this place. It seems like a tactical error, doesn't it? I'm no general, but I've pulled enough pranks to know that you always plan your escape route. Yet God sets up camp where there is no means of retreat. I think it reveals something about His strange and mysterious ways. Sometimes God leads us to a place where we have nowhere to turn but to Him; our only option is to trust Him!

So why does God wait until the very last second to make His move? Why does He let the Egyptian army get that close? Because you could make a movie about that someday! And we love those kinds of movies, don't we? Unless, of course, we're in the middle of them. Once again, the God who provides *just enough* parts the Red Sea *just in time*.

Praying hard is trusting that God will fight our battles for us. It's the way we take our hands off the challenges we face and put them into the hands of God Almighty. And He can handle them. The hard thing is keeping our hands off.

When Union Station closed, I wanted to solve the problem, but I couldn't. All I could do was stand still. I had never felt more helpless as a leader, but I had never felt more energized as well. I felt like Moses as I stood before our congregation that day and stood on this promise: "I don't know what we're going to do, but I do know what we're not going to do. We're not going to be afraid. We're going to stand still. And we're going to see the deliverance of the Lord."

And God delivered.

Less than a year after closing that door, God opened two sets of doors at the Gala Theatre in Columbia Heights and Potomac Yard in Crystal City, our fifth and sixth locations. That closed door prompted a search for property that led to us purchasing *the last piece of property on Capitol Hill*. And what I didn't know then is that those closed doors at Union Station would lead to the biggest miracle in the history of National Community Church. God opened a door that had a dead bolt on it.

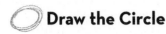 ## Draw the Circle

1. Have there been times in the past where God has not come through for you as you thought he should? How did this affect you and your relationship with God? Did you find yourself feeling distant toward God, or did you draw closer to Him and become more trusting and reliant upon Him?

2. You can't pray for open doors if you aren't willing to accept closed doors, because one leads to the other. Why is this so important to know as we pray and believe God to answer? How have some of God's no's to your prayers been some of the greatest answers you've received?

3. In what areas of your life do you need to stand still and trust in God to fight for you?

Part 3

The Third Circle —
Think Long

Toward the end of his life, Honi the circle maker was walking down a dirt road when he saw a man planting a carob tree. Always the inquisitive sage, Honi questioned him. "How long will it take this tree to bear fruit?" The man replied, "Seventy years." Honi said, "Are you quite sure you will live another seventy years to eat its fruit?" The man replied, "Perhaps not. However, when I was born into this world, I found many carob trees planted by my father and grandfather. Just as they planted trees for me, I am planting trees for my children and grandchildren so they will be able to eat the fruit of these trees."

This incident led to an insight that changed the way Honi prayed. He realized that praying is planting. Each prayer is like a seed that gets planted in the ground. It disappears for a season, but it eventually bears fruit that blesses future generations. In fact, our prayers bear fruit forever. Prayer is a timeless seed.

Even when we die, our prayers don't. Each prayer takes on a life, an eternal life, of its own. I know this because of the moments in my life when the Holy Spirit has reminded me that the prayers of my grandparents are being answered in my life right now. Their prayers outlived them.

Prayer is the inheritance we receive and the legacy we leave. Honi the circle maker didn't just pray the prayer that saved a generation. His perennial prayers were answered in the next generation too. His grandson, Abba Hilkiah, inherited the prayer legacy his grandfather left. During droughts, Israel came to his doorstep, and Hilkiah would go up on to his rooftop to pray for rain, just as his grandfather had done.

When we pray, our prayers exit our own reality of space and time. They have no time or space restrictions because the God who answers them exists outside of the space and time He created. You never know when His timeless answer will reenter the atmosphere of our lives! Even if you're in eighth grade or on your way to college, it's never too early to start praying for your future spouse or future children. Never underestimate His ability to show up anytime, anyplace, anyhow. And He answers our prayers more than once. He answers them forever. The problem, of course, is that we want immediate results. Forever is fine, but we want answers instantly.

When the Russian comedian Yakov Smirnoff immigrated to the United States (don't stereotype — Russians can be funny too!), he said that the thing he loved most about America were the grocery stores. He said, "I'll never forget walking down one of the aisles and seeing powdered milk; just add water and you get milk. Right next to it was powdered orange juice; just add water and you get orange juice. Then I saw baby powder, and I thought to myself, *What a country!*"

We live in a quick-fix, real-time culture. Between the Facebook feeds, Twitter, and 4G notifications, we're always in the know, always in the now. By the time this book is published, there'll be 5G! We want to reap the second after we sow, but this isn't the way it works with dreaming big and praying hard. What we're missing today is patience and forethought.

Because we're surrounded by technologies that make our lives faster and easier, we tend to think about spirituality in "real time" and expect "instant gratification." But almost all spiritual realities in Scripture are described in *longer* and *harder* agricultural terms. We want things to happen at the speed of light instead of the speed of a seed planted in the ground. We want our dreams to become reality overnight. We want our prayers answered immediately, if not sooner. But the key to dreaming big and praying hard is *thinking long*. Become a carob-tree planter! Instead of thinking in seven-day cycles, think in terms of seventy-year timelines.

On the Swedish island Visingsö, there's a mysterious forest of oak trees; mysterious because oak trees aren't indigenous to the island, and its origin was unknown for more than a century. Then in 1980, the Swedish Navy received a letter from the Forestry Department reporting that their requested ship lumber was ready. The Navy didn't even know it had ordered any lumber. After a little historical research, it was discovered that in 1829, the Swedish Parliament, recognizing that it takes oak trees 150 years to mature and anticipating a shortage of lumber at the turn of the twenty-first century, ordered that 20,000 oak trees be planted on Visingsö and protected for the Navy.[1]

That's what I call thinking long.

One dimension of thinking long is *thinking different*, and prayer is the key to both. Prayer doesn't just change circumstances; more important, it changes *us*. It doesn't just alter external realities; it alters internal realities so that we see out of a different lens. It gives us peripheral vision. It corrects our nearsightedness. It enables us to see beyond our circumstances, beyond ourselves, and beyond time.

It's not enough to dream big and pray hard. You also have to think long. If you don't, you'll experience high degrees of discouragement. Why? Because we tend to overestimate what we can accomplish in a year. Of course, we also tend to underestimate what we can accomplish in a decade. Bill Gates, the founder of Microsoft, said that! The bigger the vision the harder you'll have to pray and the longer you'll have to think. But if you keep circling, it'll come to pass in God's time.

The 20/20 vision of National Community Church is twenty locations by the year 2020. This isn't just dreaming big; it's thinking long. When I get discouraged, nine times out of ten it's because I've lost my carob-tree perspective. The solution? Think long. I have to remind myself of God's power, which knows no space-time limitations. I have to remind myself of God's faithfulness to answer my prayers, even after I am long gone.

Chapter 12

Long and Boring

I recently had the honor of giving the opening prayer at the annual benefit for the International Justice Mission at the Omni Shoreham in Washington, DC. You could probably care less about all these conferences, I know, but I have to set this one up. My friend, the founder of IJM, Gary Haugen, shared the story of a thirteen-year-old girl who was miraculously rescued out of a brothel in the Philippines. It's hard to hear about the horrors she endured, especially when you have a thirteen-year-old daughter. Then Gary showed a picture of her smiling face.

Only God.

He is the God who heals hearts and restores smiles.

Like most girls enslaved in the absolute darkness of sex trafficking, she wasn't allowed outside. Ever. Imagine not seeing the light of day or feeling the warmth of the sun for years on end. Then IJM's legal efforts rescued her.

I'll never forget the way Gary described it. You've probably never heard this song, but he used lyrics from "The Book of Love" to illustrate this:

The book of love is long and boring ... It's full of charts and facts and figures ... But I love it when you read to me.

Gary then used the phrase from those lyrics — "long and boring" — to describe the process of rescuing the young girl out of that brothel. It took fifty long and boring trips to a courthouse twelve hours away from the IJM office. It took 6,100 long and boring hours of filing and re-filing paperwork, which of course, the young girl couldn't pay a penny of. And who knows how many long and boring prayer circles were drawn around that brothel and around that girl.

Praying through is long and boring, but it's the price you pay for miracles. And no matter how long and boring it is, you can't put a price on a girl rescued from darkness and literally brought into the light. There is nothing boring about that, but very few of us are willing to love that long or pray that hard.

Like any good lawyer, the lawyers at IJM know how to work like it depends on them. What makes them so extraordinary is they also know how to pray like it depends on God. If you're willing to dream big *and* pray hard *and* think long, you might just bring kings to their knees and shut the mouths of lions. It's the triple threat.

Stop, Drop, and Pray

I'm sure you're going nuts with my property and lawyer talk, so now I'll talk about art. One of my favorite paintings at the National Gallery of Art is the larger-than-life portrait of Daniel in the Lions' Den by Sir Peter Paul Rubens. Daniel is ripped, to the point of steroid-suspicion (and who knows, maybe it's an accurate depiction), but far greater than his external physique was his internal fortitude. His persistence quotient was unequalled, as evidenced by his habit of getting on his knees three times a day and praying through an open window toward Jerusalem. Even when King Darius outlawed prayer, Daniel continued to stop, drop, and pray three times a day.

> *Now when Daniel learned that the decree had been published, he went home to his upstairs room where the windows opened toward Jerusalem. Three times a day he got down on his knees and prayed, giving thanks to his God, just as he had done before.*[1]

Few people prayed with more consistency or intensity than Daniel. I bet he prayed *even more* when it was illegal. He continued to pray even though he knew his dream of rebuilding Jerusalem wouldn't be fulfilled during his lifetime. He prayed toward the city that he knew he would never see with his physical eyes, yet he saw it with his spiritual eyes. Daniel prophesied that it would take "seventy years" for the destruction of Jerusalem to come to an end.[2]

Is it possible for man to dream continuously for seventy years?

You tell me, because Daniel did just that. He never stopped dreaming big or praying hard, because he was thinking long. That's what prophets do. Daniel was thinking in terms of millennia. His prayers and prophecies were the seeds in our salvation, and we reap these blessings until Christ returns.

What's so impressive to me about Daniel is that he knew his prayers wouldn't be answered for seventy years, but he prays with a sense of urgency. As a procrastinator, I would have been tempted to wait until the last week of the sixty-ninth year to even *start* praying. But somehow, he had the ability to pray with urgency about things that weren't even urgent. That's another important dimension of thinking long.

Drawing prayer circles often feels like a long and boring process, and it can be frustrating when you feel like you've been circling forever. You start to wonder if God really hears or really cares. Sometimes His silence is deafening. We circle the health of our loved ones. We circle all the "why" questions we don't have answers to. We circle the dream. But it doesn't seem to be making a difference. What do you do? My advice: Stop, drop, and pray. Keep circling. Circle for seventy years if you have to! What else are you going to do? Where else are you going to turn? What other options do you have? Pray through.

We live in a culture that overvalues fifteen minutes of fame and undervalues lifelong faithfulness. I think we have it backward. Just as our greatest successes often come on the heels of our greatest failures, our greatest answers to prayer often come on the tail end of our longest and most boring prayers. But if you pray long and boring prayers, your life will be anything but boring. Your life will turn into the spiritual adventure it was destined to be. Lifelong faithfulness pays. And it pays well! It won't necessarily get you where you want to go, but it will get you through. It got Daniel out of the lions' den! He didn't just dial up a little last minute 911 prayer, he was faithful in prayer through his life, so of course God was going to answer his prayer!

Sleepless Nights

Daniel's sleepover in the lions' den had to be the longest night of his life. He didn't sleep a wink. Going into it, it seemed like the worst (and last) thing that would ever happen to him. Coming out of it, it proved to be the best thing that ever happened to him. His faith didn't just shut the mouths of lions; his faith brought a king and kingdom to its knees. Plus his picture wound up hanging in the National Gallery of Art.

You're a teenager, which means you probably *love* sleeping. We all love a good night's sleep, but sleepless nights can define our lives. If you're going to bring kings to their knees or shut the mouths of lions, sometimes you need to pull an all-nighter. I'm more and more convinced that the biggest difference between success and failure, both spiritually and in your future, is the wake-up time on your alarm clock. If you snooze, you lose. But if you pray through, God will come through as surely as the sun will rise.

I'm sure most of you have babysat before. Ever babysit a baby with *colic*? Some of the longest nights of my life were some of the sleepless nights when Parker was a baby. He had colic and just cried for no reason. Enough said. The only thing that would quiet him was running water. So we sat by the bathtub for hours and racked up the water bill. The charge was so high the water company thought there was a mistake. Nope. Just a crying baby!

Crying babies are great for the prayer life. Those were some long and boring prayers, but now that we're seeing them answered in his life as a teenager, I wouldn't trade those sleepless nights for anything in the world.

How You Get There

Besides a new baby, I was trying to pastor a newborn church as well. Those sleepless nights were always interesting too. We had one member of the church in particular who needed a lot of counseling. And it was always in the wee hours of the morning. (Maybe you have a friend who tends to do the same thing — texting at all hours of the night.) One time he called my home phone at four in the morning, genuinely concerned that he was Jesus. No kidding. I reassured him that I knew Jesus, and he wasn't him. I told him I'd be happy to give him a few good reasons after a few more hours of sleep. Of course, Parker started crying right after I hung up.

When I was starting out as a church planter, I didn't want it to be a long and boring job. I wanted to pastor a thousand people by the time I turned thirty. When I was starting out as an author, I didn't want it to be the slow climb of an unknown writer out of obscurity. I wanted to write a *New York Times* bestseller. I'm a typical Type-A personality. I want to get where I'm going as quickly as possible. But as I look back on my journey, I am genuinely grateful that NCC didn't grow as quickly as I wanted it to. I'm not sure I would have survived if the church had thrived too soon. I am genuinely grateful that it took a dozen years and a half dozen unfinished manuscripts to finally publish my first book, *In a Pit with a Lion on a Snowy Day*. If I had written it at twenty-five instead of thirty-five, it would have been all theory and no substance.

I love what God is doing at NCC right now. But I wouldn't trade the days when our monthly income was $2,000, when we would start services with six people, or when we met in a school cafeteria without air-conditioning. Those difficult days taught us to pray hard and forced us to think long.

I love no-agenda days. Every once in a while, we all need a day with nothing to do, but those aren't the days we're going to celebrate at the end of our lives. We won't even remember those days. What we'll remember are the days when we had everything to do, and with God's help, we did it. We won't remember the things that came easy; we'll remember the things that came hard. We'll remember the miracles on the far side of "long and boring."

Hike the Inca Trail sometime. But make sure you *hike* it! It's one of the hardest things I've ever done. It took four days to navigate a trail that was breathtaking because of its beauty and literally breathtaking because of its elevation. It was almost dawn on the fourth day when we finally arrived at the Sun Gate and got our first glimpse of Machu

Picchu. It has to be one of the most spectacular places on the planet to watch the sunrise.

We had already hiked close to thirty sheer miles over three days. That's ten miles a day climbing and falling thousands of feet in elevation. The last leg of the journey, from the Sun Gate to the mountaintop city of Machu Picchu, took about an hour. By the time we arrived, the city was already swarming with tourists who had taken a bus to the top. It was easy to smell who was who. We looked and smelled like we had just hiked four days to get there; the tourists looked like they had just eaten their over-easy eggs and washed 'em down with a cup of coffee.

At first I felt sorry for myself — we had to hike four days to get here! Then I felt sorry for them. We saw it through "Inca eyes" because we got there the way they did. We walked their trail. Ancient ruins shouldn't be arrived at easily. Neither should ancient truths. That experience taught me something that's true in all of life: It's not just where you end up that's important; it's how you get there.

The harder the better.

It's true in life; it's true in prayer.

Deep Roots

Who are your heroes? Who do you look up to? One of my greatest heroes was my father-in-law, Bob Schmidgall. In fact, this book is dedicated to him. I wrote *a* book on prayer, but he wrote *the* book. He founded Calvary Church in Naperville, Illinois, and pastored there for more than thirty years. The church grew from one member to thousands of members and became one of the leading missions-giving churches in America. The greatest lesson I learned from him is this: If you plant yourself in one place and let your roots grow deep, there is no limit to what God can do. His example of longevity inspired one of my life goals: Pastor one church for forty-plus years. And his legacy of generosity inspired another: Lead National Community Church to give $25,000,000 to missions.

My father-in-law grew up on a farm in central Illinois, which meant he had a carob-tree perspective. It also meant he got up very early in the morning. He was one of the godliest men I've ever known, and I think it's because he got up at ungodly hours to pray. He spent an hour on his knees before the rest of the world even woke up. On good days, he had also read three newspapers and logged two miles on the treadmill! My mother-in-law once told me that she had to reinforce the knees on his pants because they were always the first thing to go. For thirty years, he planted himself in one place. For thirty years, he planted seeds. For thirty years, he let his roots grow deep.

One of the longest and hardest days of my life was the day of his funeral, a few days after his shocking death at the age of fifty-five. Thousands of people came to pay their respects, some of whom had never even met him but whose lives had been indirectly impacted by the sermons he preached or the prayers he prayed. We met people who put their faith in Christ while listening to one of his radio messages. We met people whose mom or dad, son or daughter, brother or sister started following Christ at his church. Even now, when I travel and speak at leadership conferences across the country, it's rare that I don't meet someone who was touched by his ministry, even though he died thirteen years ago. His lasting prayers are still bearing fruit like a carob tree.

After the funeral service, our family exited the side door of the sanctuary and got into a car right behind the hearse at the head of the funeral procession. As we drove down Route 59 from Calvary Church to Naperville Cemetery, I looked in the rearview mirror and saw the longest line of cars I had ever seen. According to the Naperville police, cars were still pulling out of the church parking lot as we pulled into the cemetery five miles away.

That's what dreaming big, praying hard, and thinking long looks like. His legacy is a long love. His legacy is the stop, drop, and pray. His legacy is a lot of early mornings and some sleepless nights.

On Call

Our family started attending Calvary Church when I was in eighth grade. It was already a megachurch with thousands of members, but my father-in-law had an amazing memory for names and faces. If he met you once, he would remember your name forever. Despite the size of the church, he never lost his shepherd's heart. He had a warm spirit that gave him an air of accessibility. Maybe that's why my parents felt like they could call him at two in the morning after my doctor issued a code blue and half a dozen nurses came rushing into my hospital room. I thought I was taking my last breath.

My mom stayed by my side while my dad called information and got a home phone number for the Schmidgalls. In less than ten minutes, my future father-in-law was at my bedside in his black double-breasted superman suit that I would later swear he slept in.

He was a large man with large hands. They looked more like meat hooks than hands. And when he prayed for people, his hands would envelop their head like a skullcap. When he laid his hands on my head, I remember thinking that there is no way God won't answer his prayer. He had a familiarity with God that was disarming. He had a faith in God that was reassuring.

He could have called a staff member to make the visit. He didn't. He could have waited until morning. He didn't. He settled for a short night's sleep on short notice to pray for a thirteen-year-old kid who was fighting for his life. Little did he know that this thirteen-year-old kid would one day marry his daughter! Little did he know that this thirteen-year-old kid would one day give him his first grandchild, a colicky baby boy named Parker. There is no way he could have ever known, but that's the magnificent mystery of prayer.

You never know who you're praying for. You never know how or when God will answer your prayers. But if you pray long and boring prayers, God will give you some exciting answers. If you're willing to interrupt your sleep cycle, your dreams might just come true.

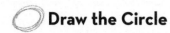 **Draw the Circle**

1. Prayer doesn't just change our circumstances; it changes us. Why is this so important for us to understand?

2. We live in a culture that overvalues fifteen minutes of fame and undervalues lifelong faithfulness. Agree or disagree? Why? How does this affect your ability to think long-term and pray through long and boring seasons of prayer?

3. What are some things that have come hard in your life? What are some things that have come easy? Which do you most treasure and believe led to your greatest growth? Why?

Chapter 13

The Greatest of Them All

1931 was a long and boring year. As you probably know from US History section 1, the stock market crash of 1929 plunged America into the depths of the Great Depression, and most businesses struggled to stay afloat. Among the struggling businessmen was a hotelier named Conrad Hilton. Americans weren't traveling, and hotels were suffering. Hilton was borrowing money from a bellhop so he could eat.

It was during those difficult days of the Depression that Hilton came across a photograph of the Waldorf Astoria in New York City. The Waldorf was the holy grail of hotels. Six kitchens, two hundred chefs, five hundred waiters, and two thousand rooms. That's massive! It even had its own private hospital and railroad. Hilton observed that 1931 was "an outrageous time to dream." But the economic crisis didn't keep him from dreaming big, praying hard, or thinking long. Hilton snipped the pic of the Waldorf out of the magazine and wrote across it, "the greatest of them all." Then he placed the photograph under the glass top of his desk. Every time Hilton sat down at his desk, his dream was staring him in the face.

Nearly two decades came and went. America emerged from the Great Depression and entered the Second World War. All the while, Hilton kept circling the Waldorf. Every time he walked by the Waldorf, he tipped his hat in honor to his dream.

Needless to say, Hilton acquired an impressive portfolio of hotels, including the Roosevelt in New York City and the Mayflower in Washington, DC, but the Queen, as he called the Waldorf, eluded him. Several attempts to purchase the hotel failed, but Hilton kept circling. Finally, on October 12, 1949, eighteen years after drawing a circle around his dream, Hilton made his move. He purchased 249,024 shares of the Waldorf Corporation and crowned his collection of hotels with the Queen.

How did he do it?

Well, Hilton definitely had some mad business and negotiation skills. He was a hardworking visionary. But a lot of people are like that, so what made him so successful? I think the true answer is revealed in his autobiography. It's the answer he learned from his mother, who had prayed circles around her son. In Hilton's own words, "My mother had one answer for everything. Prayer!"

When Conrad was a young boy, his horse, Chiquita, died. He was devastated and demanded an answer. His mother's answer was the answer to everything: "Go and pray, Connie ... Take all your problems to Him. He has answers when we don't."[1] That lesson was not lost on him as a young boy or as an old man. For eighteen long and boring years, Hilton worked like it depended on him and prayed like it depended on God. Then his persistence paid off.

The final section of Hilton's autobiography is titled "Pray Consistently and Confidently." Here Hilton provides a brief summary of his approach to business — essentially his approach to everything in life: "In the circle of successful living, prayer is the hub that holds the wheel together. Without our contact with God we are nothing. With it, we are 'a little lower than the angels, crowned with glory and honor.'"[2]

The next time you stay in a Hilton or wonder how in the world Paris Hilton came into all that "family money," remember that long before it was bricks and mortar, it was a bold prayer. It was a long shot and definitely a long thought. I especially love the fact that Hilton tipped his hat to the Waldorf whenever he walked by. He showed respect and humility in the face of a daunting dream. When you dream big, pray hard, and think long, you know your time will eventually come.

To Their Knees

Daniel ranks as one of the most brilliant minds the ancient world has ever known. He was a Renaissance man two thousand years before the Renaissance. He was a genius philosopher and scientist. He could explain riddles and solve problems unlike anyone in his generation, and no one could dream or interpret dreams like Daniel. But the thing that set him apart wasn't his IQ. Daniel prayed circles around the greatest superpower on earth, and because he got on his knees, he brought kings and kingdoms to their knees.

Physical posture is an important part of prayer. It's like a prayer within a prayer. Posture is related to prayer like tone is related to communication. You've probably heard plenty about tone from your parents! If words are what you say, then posture is how you say it. There's a reason that Scripture recommends a wide variety of postures such as kneeling, falling on one's face, the laying on of hands, and anointing someone's head with oil. Physical postures help posture our hearts and minds.

When I extend out my hands in worship, it symbolizes my surrender to God. Sometimes I'll raise a clenched fist to celebrate what Christ has accomplished for me on the cross and declare the victory He's won. We do it after a great play, so why not during a great song?

During the most recent Lenten season, Parker and I got up a half hour earlier than normal to allow a little extra time to read Scripture. We also decided we would get on our knees when we prayed. The physical posture of kneeling, coupled with a humble heart, is the most powerful position on earth. I'm not sure that the kneeling position betters my batting average in prayer, but it gets me in the right stance! All I know is this: Humility honors God, and God honors humility. Why not kneel? It certainly can't hurt.

There's nothing magical about laying hands on people or kneeling or anointing, but there is something biblical about it. There's also something mystical about it. When we practice these prescribed postures, we are doing what's been done for thousands of years, and part of thinking long is appreciating the timeless traditions that connect us to our spiritual ancestors.

Tip the Hat

I love the detailed description of Daniel's prayer posture. The nuances are not insignificant. He prayed three times a day. He went upstairs.

He got down on his knees. And he opened a window toward Jerusalem. It's the open window that intrigues me. Even when prayer is outlawed, he made no effort to conceal his actions. I bet he opened the window a little wider and prayed a little louder. The question, of course, is *why* he opened a window toward Jerusalem in the first place.

It wasn't like God couldn't hear him if the window was closed. It wasn't like God's answer depended on his principal direction, but facing Jerusalem kept Daniel pointed in the direction of his *dream*. His physical posture mirrored his mental posture. It was his way of staying focused and on-target. It was his way of keeping the dream front and center. It was his way of circling the promise. Opening his window toward Jerusalem was Daniel's way of tipping his hat at the Waldorf.

There is something powerful about being in proximity to the person, place, or thing you are praying for. If there wasn't, my future father-in-law would have just prayed over the phone and gone back to bed. Sometimes physical contact creates a spiritual connection. Nearness to your dreams and prayers can create intimacy with them. Drawing a prayer circle is a physical way of marking territory — God's territory.

I spent many a Saturday night praying on the plaza in front of Union Station when we held services there. Then on Sunday mornings, I walked the aisles, laying hands on every single theater seat.

Since I introduced our congregation to Honi the circle maker, I've heard dozens of different applications. There are lots of schools and homes in Washington, DC, that have been circled in prayer. In each instance, praying in proximity made these prayers more than just a "going through the motions" event. Like the promise given to Joshua, "I will give you every place where you set your foot," it's a way of exercising the authority God has given us as His children.[3]

Some prayer circles are invisible, but some are physical. There are several thousand Bibles planted all the way around Washington, DC. Very few people know about it, but the group that planted them felt like God wanted them to demonstrate their faith by establishing a perimeter. I'm not recommending you do the same exact thing, but sometimes you need to do something physical to symbolize your faith.

For many years, we laid hands on the walls at 205 F Street, praying that God would give us 201 F Street. When God answered those prayers, we laid our hands on the other side of those walls. We climbed down twenty-foot ladders and held a prayer meeting in the concrete foundation of our future coffeehouse. We didn't just lay hands on those walls; we circled the promises of God by writing them on the walls. Those walls are primed with prayers and prophecies. We have long since covered them with acoustic treatments in our performance space, but they're ever present.

We did a similar thing with our Barracks Row location. We had the congregation write prayers and circle promises on the floor there with Sharpies after a worship service one night. Some are in Latin, some are in Hebrew, and most are in English, but all of them are inscribed on the floor that is now covered by carpet.

If there's something you feel called to do in order to make a prayer promise physical and real, maybe it's time you gave it a try.

Spiritual Priming

One of the summer jobs I had as a teenager was painting, but it didn't last long because, quite frankly, I wasn't very good. I got fired in less than a week. I did learn one thing though: priming is an important part of painting. If you don't have the right primer, you'll be painting forever. If you're painting the wall a light color, you need a light primer; if you're painting the wall a dark color, you need a dark primer. It may seem like the primer is unnecessary. It may seem like a primer takes more time and more work, but it actually increases quality while decreasing the quantity of work.

Hold that thought.

Over the last few decades, New York University psychologist John Bargh has conducted priming experiments on unsuspecting students.[4] One of the experiments involved a scrambled-sentence test. The first test was sprinkled with rude words like *disturb*, *bother*, and *intrude*. The second test was sprinkled with polite words like *respect*, *considerate*, and *yield*. In both cases, the subjects thought they were taking tests measuring intelligence. None of the subjects picked up on the word trend consciously, but it primed them subconsciously.

After taking the five-minute test, students were asked to walk down the hall and talk to the person running the experiment about their next assignment. An actor was strategically engaged in conversation with the experimenter when the students would arrive. The goal was to see how long it would take students to interrupt.

Bargh wanted to know if the students who were primed with polite words would take longer to interrupt the conversation than those primed with rude words. He suspected that the subconscious priming would have a slight effect, but the effect was profound in measurable terms. The group primed with rude words interrupted, on average, after five minutes, but 82 percent of those primed with polite words never interrupted at all. Who knows how long they would have patiently and politely waited if the researchers hadn't given the test a ten-minute time limit.

Is that crazy or what?

Our minds are subconsciously primed by everything that is happening all the time. It's a testament to the fact that our minds are "fearfully and wonderfully made."[5] It also testifies to the fact that we had better be good filters of the things we allow into our eyes and ears. Everything we see and hear is priming us in a positive or negative way. That's one reason I believe in starting the day in God's Word. It doesn't just prime our minds; it also primes our hearts. It's doesn't just prime us spiritually; it also primes us emotionally and relationally. When we read the words that the Holy Spirit inspired, it tunes us to His voice and primes us for His promptings. It allows us to be more patient emotionally and have clearer perspective in our relationships.

A few years ago, two Dutch researchers did a similar priming experiment with a group of students by asking them forty-two questions from the Trivial Pursuit board game. Half of the students were told to take five minutes to contemplate what it would mean to be a university professor and write down everything that came to mind. The other group was told to sit and think about soccer for five minutes.

The professor group got 55.6 percent of the questions right.

The soccer group got 42.6 percent of the questions right.[6]

The people in the professor group weren't any smarter than the people who were in the soccer group. And if watching sports decreased intelligence, I'd be an idiot. Especially during football season! The professor group was simply in a smart frame of mind! Maybe half of being smart is believing you're smart ... food for thought. (Particularly before your next test.)

What does that have to do with prayer?

Prayer is priming. Prayer puts us in a spiritual frame of mind. Prayer helps us see and seize the God-ordained opportunities that are all around us all the time.

Larks and Owls

Daniel was so primed with prayer that it didn't just sanctify him, he felt that he needed to prime Nebuchadnezzar too! Daniel discerned the king's dream because he could read his mind. It's almost as though prayer gives us a sixth sense.

Somewhere near the intersection of science and spirituality is a paradigm-shifting principle best seen in the priming exercise practiced by King David:

In the morning, LORD, you hear my voice;
   in the morning I lay my requests before you
   and wait expectantly.[7]

One of the reasons that many people don't feel an intimacy with God is because they don't have a daily rhythm with God; they have a *weekly* rhythm. Would that work with your closest friends or possibly your family? It doesn't work in God's family either. We need to establish a daily rhythm in order to have a daily relationship with God. The best way to do that is to begin the day in prayer.

The most important ten minutes of my day are the ten minutes I spend reading Scripture and praying with my kids at the beginning of the day. Nothing even comes in a close second. It sets the tone for the day. It opens the lines of communication. It gets us started on the right foot.

I realize that there are larks and owls. Owls are just getting started when the rest of the world is winding down; larks are way too happy way too early. But whether you're an owl or a lark, you still need to begin the day in prayer for the purposes of priming.

I love the determination in David's voice: "In the morning, LORD, you hear my voice." That's all it takes, doesn't it? It's hard to get up early, but that is what makes praying hard so hard. It's the same determination that I see in Daniel.

Then David declares, "I lay my requests before you and wait expectantly." Most of us just wait; David waited expectantly. There's a big difference.

Our biggest shortcoming is low expectations. We underestimate how good and how great God is by 15.5 billion light-years. The solution to that is just prayer!

The Mystery Box

Let me sidetrack for one minute, because I love this story.

J.J. Abrams is a brilliant filmmaker who has created everything from *Lost* to *Mission Impossible III* to *Super 8*. He's a story-weaving, suspense-building genius. He's driven by the element of suspense, but why? Glad you asked.

When he was a kid, he read comic books, and one day he saw an advertisement for a "Mystery Box" in the back of one of them. It cost five dollars, which was a lot of money for a kid, but he wanted it so bad he ordered it anyway. He waited by the mailbox every day. Finally it showed up, but he couldn't bring himself to open it. He realized that the suspense of not knowing what was inside is what made the mystery so amazing. To this day, J.J. has the Mystery Box on the shelf behind his desk, unopened.

I think prayer is a lot like a mystery box. It adds suspense to our lives. And while that is sometimes stressful, it's the very thing that makes life worth living! I can't wait 'til God opens the box and reveals all the mysteries of His universe. And one of the greatest mysteries is how God hears, processes, and answers billions of prayers.

Prayer is also the way we sanctify our expectations. Laying requests before the Lord was David's way of circling the promises of God. I'm not sure whether they were written requests, but they created a category in David's mind (for future reference — his Reticular Activating System). After laying his requests before the Lord, he was primed and ready.

One way I've put this principle into practice is praying through my calendar instead of just looking through it. It's amazing what a difference it makes when I pray circles around the people I'm meeting with or spending time with.

We don't know what he did with his daily requests. Maybe he posted them on the royal refrigerator; maybe he stuck them to his throne with the ancient equivalent of a sticky note. What we do know is that they sanctified his expectations.

Quirky

Like everyone else, I have my fair share of quirks. I don't know why, but I always set my alarm clock to an even number. An odd number would totally mess me up. I always start shaving on the right side of my face. I never drive off after pumping gas without checking my left-hand rearview mirror because the last time I failed to do that, I pulled the gas hose with me. And I always take my shoes off while I write.

Even Jesus had quirks. He loved to pray early in the morning, even after a late night of ministry.[8] And He must have felt close to his Father when He hiked mountains and walked beaches. He gravitated to those places because proximity is an important part of prayer, but it goes beyond geography; I think it also has to do with genealogy.

One of my peculiarities, as you know already, is that I occasionally do devotions out of my grandfather's Bible. In fact, I started this year in the book of Daniel because I was doing a Daniel fast. Toward the end of his life, my grandfather suffered from a medical condition that caused his hands to tremble so much that his writing is pretty much scribble. But based on the number of underlinings, Daniel was one of his favorite books. I actually know it was because I've heard stories of him and his brothers and cousins sitting around the table for hours on end talking about prophecies in Daniel. They were long thinkers and long talkers.

Seeing the verses that my grandfather underlined is powerful and meaningful because it helps me get into his mind and his spirit. I hope that the promises I have circled in my Bible will help my grandchildren do the same thing.

One important dimension of prayer is finding your own ritual and routines. Just like Daniel, you need to find your open window toward Jerusalem.

I'm sure Honi the circle maker prayed in a lot of different ways at a lot of different times. He had a wide variety of prayer postures. But when he needed to pray through, he drew a circle and dropped to his knees. His inspiration for the prayer circle was Habakkuk. He simply did what the prophet Habakkuk had done:

"I will stand upon my watch, and station me within a circle."[9]

Where do you dream big? When do you pray hard? What helps you think long?

You need to identify the times, places, and practices that help you dream big, pray hard, and think long. When I want to dream big, I hang out at the National Gallery of Art. When I want to pray hard, I climb the ladder to the rooftop of Ebenezer's Coffeehouse. When I need to think long, I take the elevator up to the sixth-floor observation gallery at the National Cathedral. Those are my places. My holy ground. And you need to find that for yourself. It takes time to discover the rhythms and routines that work for you. What works for others might not work for you, and what works for you might not work for others.

One of the great dangers in writing *The Circle Maker* is the application of these prayer principles without any thought. It's not a formula; it's faith. It's not a methodology; it's theology. It honestly doesn't matter whether it's a circle, an oval, or a trapezoid. You can be in a 3D box, if you want. Drawing prayer circles is nothing more than laying our requests before God and waiting expectantly. If walking in circles helps you pray with more consistency and intensity, then make yourself dizzy; if not, then find something, find anything, that helps you pray through.

Prayer Experiment

One of NCC's great core values is that *everything is an experiment.* And because we value experimentation, our congregation feels empowered to practice ancient spiritual disciplines in new ways. It's actually pretty cool!

Several years ago, I officiated at the wedding of David and Selina. During premarital counseling, Selina told me the backstory to their love story. It was quite the experiment. Selina had a friend who used to organize prayer circles by recruiting ten people to pray for one thing for one person every day for thirty or forty or sixty days. The net results were amazing. That prayer experiment planted a seed in her spirit, and a few weeks later, she adapted the idea and came up with her own prayer experiment.

Selina recruited nine friends, and together they formed a prayer circle. They decided to pray for each other every day and focus their prayers on the greatest of prayer struggles — men. Not everybody in the prayer circle knew each other. In fact, not all of them liked each other! But God began to bond them as they prayed for each other day in and day out. They would often call each other if they felt prompted to share what the Lord was impressing on them during prayer, and it was amazing how often their prayers were perfectly targeted or timed.

At the end of forty days, the group decided to renew their prayer experiment for another forty days. The first forty days were full of spiritual attacks, but that encouraged them because it was evidence that they were doing something right. During the second forty-day period, the group saw tremendous victories in big things and little things. It was during those forty days that Selina met David, but it was the focused prayers of nine friends that prepared her to meet him. She identified some of the lies she had believed and mistakes she had made. Then she circled them in prayer while her prayer circle double-circled them.

I love this particular prayer experiment not just because I had the privilege of marrying David and Selina; I love it because it's the perfect marriage of praying hard and thinking long. It can seem far off or irrelevant to teenagers, because maybe you don't even have nine friends who are believers! Start with one. Or just find someone who you know is a believer and ask them to partner in prayer with you, even if you don't know them well. You have to start somewhere.

What would happen if you focused your prayers on one thing for one person for one month or one year? There's only one way to find out: do your own prayer experiment.

Game with Minutes

I'll end with one of the greatest prayer experiments I've heard of. On January 30, 1930, Frank Laubach began a prayer experiment he called "the game with minutes." He was dissatisfied with his intimacy with God and decided to do something about it. Laubach's question for his experiment was simple: "Can we have contact with God all the time?" He chose to make the rest of his life an experiment in answering this question.

Frank sought to break down the false beliefs that he had been taught from a young age. Then he rebuilt his prayer life from the ground up. Think about all the stereotypes about prayer. All the labels society puts on "that weird thing Christians do." Prayer isn't something we do with our eyes closed; we pray with our eyes wide open. Prayer isn't a sentence that begins with "Dear Jesus" and ends with "Amen." The best prayer doesn't even involve words at all; the best prayer is a life well lived. All of life is meant to be a prayer, just as all of life is meant to be an act of worship.

Frank described "the game with minutes" in these terms:

> We try to call Him to mind at least one second of each minute. We do not need to forget other things nor stop our work, but we invite Him to share everything we do or say or think. Hundreds of us have experimented until we have found ways to let Him share every minute of our waking hours.[10]

One of the ways that Frank played "the game with minutes" was shooting people with prayer. Some people would walk by without any reaction, but some people would do a sudden about-face and smile.

Six months into his experiment, Frank wrote these words in his prayer journal:

> Last Monday was the most completely successful day of my life to date, so far as giving my day in complete and continuous surrender to God is concerned ... I remember how as I looked at people with a love God gave, they looked back and acted as though they wanted to go with me. I felt then that for a day I saw a little of that marvelous pull that Jesus had as He walked along the road day after day "God-intoxicated" and radiant with the endless communion of His soul with God.[11]

A prayer experiment like this can turn even the most boring of biology class or workout or babysitting job into a meaningful spiritual discipline. What if we converted every problem, every opportunity, into a prayer? What if we stopped reading the news and started praying it? What if lunch with friends turned into prayer for your friends? Maybe we'd come a lot closer to our goal: praying without ceasing.

◯ Draw the Circle

1. Take a moment to pray in a new posture. To follow the Quakers' practice, begin with your hands down, symbolizing the things you need to let go of in your life. Confess your sins, let go of your past, and let go of control of your life. Then turn your hands over so they face up to receive from God. Pray to receive from the Lord what He wants to give you — joy, peace, and grace.

2. To have a daily relationship with God, we have to establish a daily rhythm with God every morning. How is your daily prayer rhythm with God? How is your daily Bible reading rhythm with God? Do you have a specific spot or place you like to go to pray? If you have not established a daily rhythm with God, how do you think your life would be different if you did?

3. What prayer experiment can you and a circle of friends commit to for thirty days? What spiritual breakthrough can you imagine this experiment will bring?

Chapter 14

The Speed of Prayer

In the world of aviation, the sound barrier was once considered the unbreakable barrier. Many engineers believed that Mach 1 represented an impenetrable wall of air, and the dozens of pilots who died trying to break the barrier solidified that belief. At low speeds, shock waves are a non-factor, but as an aircraft reaches higher speeds, there's a different set of aerodynamics.

Anyone into physics? Anyone *enjoy* physics? Because this is actually cool. When a plane approaches the speed of sound, shock waves increase and cause pilots to lose control. The buildup of air pressure in front of the aircraft causes a wave drag. And because the air on top of the wing is traveling faster than air on the bottom, due to Bernoulli's principle it typically results in a catastrophic nosedive. The British put their attempt on hold after their prototype, the Swallow, imploded at Mach .94. But that didn't keep a young American pilot named Chuck Yeager from attempting the impossible.

On October 14, 1947, a four-engine B-29 took off from Muroc Field high up in the California desert. Attached to the belly of the bomber was the Bell X-1 experimental plane. At 25,000 feet, the X-1 dropped from the fuselage, its rocket engine fired into life, and then it ascended to 42,000 feet. As the plane approached Mach 1, it began to shake violently. The challenge of controlling the plane was compounded by the fact that Yeager had broken two ribs while horseback riding two days before. He didn't tell his colleagues because he didn't want to delay history and his chance to make it. (Don't you already love this guy?) As his plane hit Mach .965, the speed indicator went haywire. At Mach .995, the g-force blurred his vision and turned his stomach. Then, just as the plane was about to disintegrate, there was the crack of a sonic boom followed by an almost instantaneous and eerie silence. The plane crossed the sound barrier. Do you understand how fast a *thing* has to be going to be moving faster than *sound*? He was shooting forward at 761 miles per hour! As he did so, the air pressure shifted from the front of the plane to the back. The shock waves that had buffeted the cockpit turned into a sea of glass. Yeager reached Mach 1.07 before cutting his engines and coming back down to earth. The unbreakable barrier had been broken.

I had the privilege of hearing Chuck Yeager recount his experiences at the Smithsonian National Air and Space Museum with Parker's Cub Scout troop a little while back. Right outside the IMAX Theater where Yeager gave the speech, the Bell X-1 is symbolically suspended in midair, along with other historic air- and spacecraft. Each one represents a breakthrough. Each one is a symbol of the impossible becoming possible. Each one is a testament to the genius and guts of the human spirit, which of course, is a gift of the Holy Spirit.

Sort of like the sound barrier, there is a faith barrier. If you want to experience a supernatural breakthrough, you have to pray through. But as you get closer to the breakthrough, it often feels like you're about to lose control, about to fall apart. That's when you need to press in and pray through. Your disappointments will create too much drag if you let them. If you allow them to, your doubts will nosedive your dreams. But if you pray through, God will come through and you'll experience a supernatural breakthrough.

Almost like a sonic boom in your spirit, there comes a moment in prayer when you know that God has answered your prayer. In that moment, your frustration and confusion give way to quiet confidence. Your spirit becomes like a sea of glass because you know it's out of your hands. Let God's pinky take care of your worries and insecurities. The natural resistance that was thwarting you turns into supernatural momentum that's propelling you.

Daniel Fast

At critical intervals in my life I've done a Daniel fast. It's called a Daniel fast because it's inspired by the intense fasts that Daniel did at critical intervals in *his* life. It's different from an absolute fast because the diet generally consists of fruits, vegetables, and water. And it's typically done with a specific goal and defined timeline in mind. It was a ten-day fast that kick-started Daniel's sudden and dramatic climb to political power; it was a twenty-one-day fast that ended with an angelic encounter.

Fasting and praying is awesome as a package deal. It's almost like those moving sidewalks that get you to your destination in like half the time. They call it *fast*ing for a reason — it has a way of fast-tracking our prayers! Because fasting is physically harder than praying, fasting is a form of praying hard. In my experience, it's the shortest distance to a breakthrough.

Listen to these words spoken to Daniel:

> *"Do not be afraid, Daniel. Since the first day that you set your mind to gain understanding and to humble yourself before your God, your words were heard, and I have come in response to them. But the prince of the Persian kingdom resisted me twenty-one days. Then Michael, one of the chief princes, came to help me, because I was detained there with the king of Persia. Now I have come to explain to you what will happen to your people in the future, for the vision concerns a time yet to come."[1]*

Can you imagine having a conversation with your guardian angel? It'll be one of our most revealing conversations when we get to heaven, but Daniel got lucky and got to have a short conversation during his lifetime. For some of us, it'll be an awfully long conversation because we kept our angel awfully busy. This is certainly true of Daniel. I can't help but wonder if they had a little side conversation about the lions' den.

Like all angelic greetings, it begins with "do not be afraid." I guess that's angel protocol. Then the angel talks about the realities of the spiritual realm in a way seen nowhere else in Scripture. The angel reveals the importance of praying through. The angel reveals the spiritual warfare being waged beyond the curtain of our consciousness. The angel reveals the way prayers are processed. Go back and read it again, because you might need to chew on that a second time.

Daniel's prayer was heard before the words even passed through his vocal chords, but it wasn't until the twenty-first day that he experienced a breakthrough because of spiritual oppression. An evil spirit (the prince of the Persian kingdom) resisted the call for angelic backup until the twenty-first day.

You probably saw this coming, but let's get counterfactual: What if Daniel had quit praying through on day twenty, hour 23, minute 59? The answer is simple: Daniel would have forfeited the miracle the day before *the day*. Those are important questions to ask because you don't want to miss miracles! I don't know where you are on the timeline between praying through and breaking through. Maybe you're at day one; maybe you're at day twenty. Either way, you can pray with a holy confidence, knowing that with each prayer circle you *are* one prayer closer. Don't give up. Just like Daniel, the answer is on the way!

Empty Stomach

There is more than one way to draw a prayer circle. In fact, sometimes it involves more than prayer. I believe that fasting is a form of circling. In fact, an empty stomach may be the most powerful prayer posture in Scripture.

Even Jesus said that some miracles are not possible via prayer. Some miracles are only accessible via prayer and fasting. It takes the combination of prayer and fasting to unlock some double dead bolts.

When I have a big decision to make, I circle it with a fast. It doesn't just purge my body; it also purges my mind and spirit. When I need a breakthrough, I circle it with a fast. It doesn't just break down the challenges I'm facing; it also breaks down the calluses in my heart.

Let's unpack some stereotypes on fasting as well. Fasting is in no way starving yourself. And it's more than a diet. Fasting from food is only one form of fasting. Our family fasted TV for an entire summer once. Maybe you need to turn the phone off for a week or put the computer away. If you're an impulsive buyer, fast buying new things. What do you think you can't live without? If it's not Jesus or your Bible — fast it!

Maybe there is something you've been praying for that you need to start fasting for. You need to take it to the next level. You need to draw a double circle by fasting for your friends or for a family member or for your school. Of course, those are vague, but I'll let you fill in the blanks with specific prayers.

I've tried to make fasting a regular routine by doing a Daniel fast at the beginning of the calendar year. During this year's Daniel fast, I felt led to pray for seven miracles. I know what you're thinking: *Is that all he ever does?* You're probably wondering if I have a fixation with the number *seven* too. I promise you, I don't. And the truth is that I'd only done this twice in my life. I don't even come close to believing for the quantity and quality of miracles that I could or should.

It had been several years since writing seven miracles on a rock, and I believed that God wanted to stretch my faith again. Instead of writing them on a rock, I downloaded the Evernote App and double-thumbed these prayer requests into my iPhone.

I was two for seven the last time. I'm five for seven this time. And these seven miracles are bigger than the last seven miracles.

One of the seven miracles I prayed for was a $1 million payoff of our mortgage on Ebenezer's Coffeehouse. During the fast, we paid off that million-dollar debt. In fact, we paid off all of our debt. And so in the past twelve months we've acquired more than $10 million in property *and* we're debt free for the first time in ten years! You've got to be tired of property miracles, but come on. Only God.

But the biggest miracles aren't even financial. The biggest miracles are the hundreds of people who have submitted their lives to the Lordship of Jesus Christ. Every baptism we have, it's almost impossible for me to read the testimonies through my tears. At our last baptism, a couple dozen NCCers publically professed their faith. We ask every baptism candidate to write out the testimony of how they came to faith in Christ, and every single one is a testament to God's sovereignty and a trophy of God's grace.

The Genesis

Now consider this: When did the breakthrough happen for Daniel? Was it the moment Daniel started circling on day one? Or was it the moment he had prayed through and experienced the angelic breakthrough on day twenty-one?

The answer is both/and. Every breakthrough has a genesis and a revelation, literally and figuratively. There is a first breakthrough and a second breakthrough. So with that in mind: Why would you work for the first breakthrough and not continue to achieve the second?

Let me retrace the circle.

"The moment you began praying, a command was given."[2]

This one revelation has the power to change your perspective on prayer. Like the other statements I've made, it can change your prayer outlook if you let it. It can encourage you to dream big, pray hard, and think long. The answer is given long before it is revealed. It's not unlike the Jericho miracle when God said He had already given them the city, past tense. Do you realize that the victory has already been won? We're still waiting for its future tense revelation, but the victory has already been won by means of the death and resurrection of Jesus Christ. *It is finished.* This isn't just when God made good on grace; it is when God made good on every promise. Every single one is yes in Christ. Past tense. Present tense. Future tense. The full revelation won't happen until His return, the return that Daniel prophesied, but the victory has already been won, once and for all, for all time.

One Resolution

Every miracle has a genesis moment.

In the first century BC, it was a circle in the sand drawn by a sage named Honi. For Moses, it was declaring that God would provide meat to eat in the middle of nowhere, even though he had no idea how. For Elijah, it was getting on his knees seven times and praying for rain. For Daniel, I think it traces back to one resolution.

Destiny is not a mystery. Good or bad, your destiny is the result of your daily decisions and defining choices.

Daniel made the decision to stop, drop, and pray three times a day. Those daily decisions add up. If you make good decisions on a daily basis, it has a build-up effect that pays big the rest of your life.

Along with daily decisions, there are defining choices. We only make a few defining decisions in life, and then we spend the rest of our lives managing them. Maybe you've made some bad decisions that have gotten you to where you don't want to be. The good news is that you're only one defining decision away from a totally different life.

Daniel makes one of those defining decisions as a teenager. It doesn't seem like a big deal, but it changes the course of his story and history. Daniel's ascent to power traces all the way back to one resolution.

Daniel resolved not to defile himself with the royal food and wine.[3]

Daniel risked his reputation by refusing the royal food. It was an insult to the king, but Daniel was more concerned about insulting *God*. Daniel knew it would violate Jewish dietary laws, and while that may not seem like a big deal, if you obey God in the little things, then God knows He can use you to do big things! Daniel did a ten-day fast that won him favor with the king's chief official and that favor led into his first job with the administration. Then "the favor of him who dwelt in the burning bush" kept opening doors via a series of promotions until Daniel was second-in-command to the king.

I wonder if Daniel ever had one of those out-of-the-spirit moments when he looked in the mirror and asked himself, "How did I even get here?" The answer: daily decisions and defining choices. Never underestimate the potential of one resolution to change your life. It can be a genesis moment. Daniel's destiny traces all the way back to one resolution not to defile himself, but making the resolution was easier than keeping it. The first step is always the hardest step. That is where prayer, coupled with fasting, comes into play.

Spirit Versus Flesh

On the eve of His crucifixion, Jesus was in Gethsemane praying hard and thinking long. The usual. You know this and how this works. He was about to face the greatest test of His life, and He knew He needed to pray through the night. His disciples were supposed to be praying, but instead they were sleeping. They probably pretended to be praying when He awakened them, but drooling and snoring are usually dead giveaways. You can hear the disappointment in Jesus's voice when He asks them, "Couldn't you men keep watch with me for *one* hour?"[4]

That challenge is worth circling. Take it literally. Take it personally.

Jesus was always coming through for the disciples, but the disciples couldn't pray through for Him. They didn't even last an hour. The disciples let Jesus down when He needed them most. It didn't just hurt Jesus; Jesus knew it would hurt them as well.

Let me play counterfactual theorist again.

I wonder if Peter would have denied Jesus if he had been praying instead of sleeping. Maybe he failed the test three times because he hadn't done his prayer homework. He wasn't primed for action! We see those three denials as three temptations, but I think it's the other way around: they were three opportunities to finally get it right. While I can't prove it, I think Peter would have passed the test if he had prayed through. But he didn't. Food for thought.

Then Jesus hits the bull's-eye:

"The spirit is willing, but the flesh is weak."[5]

Is it ever! Never were truer words spoken.

Most people have a willing spirit; it's the weak flesh that gets in the way. The problem isn't desire; the problem is power — more specifically, willpower. This is where fasting comes into play. Fasting gives you more power to pray because it's an exercise in willpower. The physical discipline gives you the spiritual discipline to pray through. An empty stomach leads to a full spirit. The combo of prayer and fasting will give you the power and willpower to pray through until you experience a breakthrough.

Escape Velocity

Chuck Yeager is awesome and breaking the sound barrier is amazing, but not nearly as amazing as what happened on July 16, 1969. That is the day Neil Armstrong, Michael Collins, and Buzz Aldrin climbed aboard Apollo 11 on Launch Pad 39A at the Kennedy Space Center. The multistage rocket itself weighed 102,907 pounds and it carried 5,625,000 pounds of propellant.

Breaking the sound barrier is one thing; exiting the earth's atmosphere is a whole other thing altogether. At takeoff, the five engines produced 7,500,000 pounds of thrust in order to exceed the gravitational pull of the planet and reach an escape velocity of 17,500 mph. But that only gets you into orbit. If you want to shoot the moon, you've got to top 25,000 mph.

Prayer is the way we escape the gravitational pull of the flesh and enter God's orbit. It's the way we escape our atmosphere and enter His space. It's the way we overcome our human limitations and enter the cosmic realm where all things are possible.

Without prayer, there is no escape. With prayer and fasting, there is no doubt. Like tandem staging, it will take you to spiritual heights you never imagined possible. You won't just escape our atmosphere; if you pray a little harder and fast a little longer, you can shoot the moon.

On Sunday, July 20, 1969, Buzz Aldrin and Neil Armstrong landed their lunar module, the Eagle, on the Sea of Tranquility. The first thing they did was celebrate Communion. Because of a lawsuit filed by Madalyn Murray O'Hair, when NASA aired the reading from Genesis by the astronauts of Apollo 8, it decided to black out that part of the broadcast. Little known fact!

Aldrin, an elder in the Presbyterian Church (USA), took out a Communion kit provided by Webster Presbyterian Church in Houston, Texas. In the one-sixth gravity, the wine curled and gracefully came up the side of the cup. Just before eating the bread and drinking the cup, Aldrin read from the gospel of John:

> "I am the vine, you are the branches; he who abides in Me and I in him, he bears much fruit, for apart from Me you can do nothing."[6]

It must be hard *not* to dream big when you're 238,857 miles from earth. It must be hard *not* to pray hard when you're traveling 25,000 miles per hour through space. It must be hard *not* to think long and think different when you're watching the earthrise from the surface of the moon.

After the greatest technological feat the world had ever known, Aldrin circled back to an agricultural metaphor about bearing fruit. It's a long way from the garden of Gethsemane to the Sea of Tranquility, both in terms of miles and in terms of years. But when you plant carob trees, you never know when or where or how they will bear fruit. But bear fruit they will, two thousand years later and 238,857 miles away. They will bear fruit from here to eternity, from here to infinity.

Draw the Circle

1. Have you ever fasted — a Daniel fast or any other? If you have, describe the experience. What were the spiritual benefits you experienced due to the fast?

2. Daniel made the daily decision to stop, drop, and pray three times a day, and the defining decision to live to please God rather than men. These changed his life and established his relationship with God. What daily decisions are you making that build your relationship with God? What defining decision have you made that has changed your life?

3. What are some areas of sin and spiritual weakness you want to overcome? How might fasting help you break the cycle by focusing your prayers to achieve escape velocity?

Chapter 15

Life Goal List

On a rainy afternoon in 1940, a fifteen-year-old dreamer named John Goddard pulled out a piece of paper and wrote "My Life List" at the top. In one afternoon, he wrote down 127 life goals. It's amazing what can be accomplished in one afternoon, isn't it? By the time he turned fifty, John Goddard had accomplished 108 of his 127 goals. And this is no Internet Bucket List.

- ☑ *Milk a poisonous snake.*
- ☑ *Skin-dive to forty feet and hold breath two-and-a-half minutes underwater.*
- ☑ *Learn jujutsu.*
- ☑ *Study primitive culture in Borneo.*
- ☑ *Land on and take off from an aircraft carrier.*
- ☑ *Run a mile in five minutes.*
- ☑ *Go on a church missions trip.*
- ☑ *Retrace the travels of Marco Polo and Alexander the Great.*
- ☑ *Learn French, Spanish, and Arabic.*
- ☑ *Play the flute and violin.*
- ☑ *Photograph Victoria Falls in Rhodesia.*
- ☑ *Light a match with a .22 rifle.*
- ☐ *Climb Mount Kilimanjaro.*
- ☐ *Study Komodo dragons on the island of Komodo.*
- ☑ *Build a telescope.*
- ☑ *Read the Bible from cover to cover.*
- ☑ *Circumnavigate the globe.*

☑ *Visit the birthplace of Grandfather Sorenson in Denmark.*
☑ *Publish an article in* National Geographic *magazine.*

My favorite Goddard goal is one he never achieved: *Visit the moon.* Now that's what I call dreaming big and thinking long. He set the goal before anyone had ever escaped the earth's atmosphere!

John didn't accomplish every goal he set. He never climbed Mount Kilimanjaro, and his quest to visit every country in the world fell a few countries short. There were also some disappointments along the way. His goal of studying Komodo dragons (the world's largest living lizards) was thwarted when his boat broke down twenty miles offshore. So John hasn't accomplished all of his goals, but I doubt he would have accomplished half of what he did if he hadn't set the goals in the first place. After all, you'll never achieve the goals you don't set.

The brain is a goal-seeking organism. Setting a goal creates structural tension in your brain, which will seek to close the gap between where you are and where you want to be, who you are and who you want to be. If you don't set goals, your mind will become stagnant. Goal setting is good stewardship of your right-brain imagination. It's also great for your prayer life!

When I first read John Goddard's list of life goals, I was moved to come up with my own life goal list. While I started more than a decade ago, my list of 100-plus is still just a rough draft. Every year I check a few goals off the list; I also add new goals along the way.

Dreams with Deadlines

What do life goals have to do with dreaming big? For that matter, what does goal setting have to do with praying hard and thinking long? The answer is everything. Goal setting is a great way of doing all three at the same time.

Goals are the cause and effect of *praying hard.* The more you pray, the more God-sized goals you'll be inspired to go after. Prayer is the only way you'll accomplish a God-sized goal. Simply put, prayers naturally turn into goals, and goals naturally turn into prayers. Goals give you a prayer target. And prayer gives your goals wheels!

In their innovative book *Built to Last,* Jim Collins and Jerry Porras introduced the acronym BHAGs (Big Hairy Audacious Goals).[1] I liked that, but I've substituted a P for the G. I think of my God-sized goals as Big Hairy Audacious Prayers (BHAPs). They force me to work like it depends on me and pray like it depends on God.

Goals are a great way of *thinking long.* I have checked off nearly a quarter of my life goal list. Some of them, like speaking for an NFL chapel or coaching a sports team for each of my kids, I've checked off numerous times. But a few of my life goals will take a lifetime to achieve. It might take until I'm seventy-five to write twenty-five books. I can't pay for my grandchildren's college education until I have grandchildren. And I have no idea when I'll be part of baptizing three thousand people in the same place at the same time, like the day of Pentecost, but it's on my life goal list. And that's why they are *life* goals. They might take a lifetime to achieve, but they're worth waiting for and working for.

Finally, setting goals is a practical way of *dreaming big.* If prayer is the genesis of dreams, then goals are the revelation. In other words, prayer is breakthrough number one, goal setting is breakthrough number two! Goals are well-defined dreams that are measurable. Getting in shape is not a goal; it's a wish. Running a half marathon, however, is a goal because you know you've accomplished it when you cross the finish line. It's more satisfying that way too.

Goals are dreams with deadlines. But I like to think they're more like *life*lines. Without a deadline, I wouldn't have accomplished half of anything I've done because I'm both a procrastinator and a perfectionist. And that's why so many dreams go unaccomplished. If you don't give your dream a deadline, it will be dead before you know it. Deadlines keep dreams alive. Deadlines bring dead dreams back to life.

I dreamed of writing a book for thirteen years, but I didn't put myself on a timeline and the lack of deadline came close to killing my dream. Then I set a goal of writing a book before my thirty-fifth birthday. That target gave me something to shoot at so I was able to finish my first manuscript and accomplish a life goal.

Visualization

"Show me your vision, and I'll show you your future."

I was twenty-one when I heard those words. And I'll never forget them. They impacted me in a deep way.

Scripture says that without a vision, people perish.[2] But with a vision, people prosper. The future is always created twice. The first creation happens in your mind as you envision the future; the second creation happens when you literally flesh it out.

Vision starts with visualization. In 1995, Alvaro Pascual-Leone did a study validating the importance of visualization. A group of volunteers practiced a five-finger piano exercise while neurotransmitters monitored their brain activity. As expected, neuroimaging revealed that the motor cortex (which controls physical activities like walking and writing and humming) was active while practicing the exercise. Then researchers told the participants to mentally rehearse the piano exercise in their mind. The motor cortex was just as active while they imagined playing the exercise as it was during physical practice. Researchers came to this conclusion: imagined movements are mentally the same as their physical counterparts.

So mental rehearsal is just as important as physical practice, according to the study. I think this just goes to show the importance well-defined dreams. In Star Wars lingo: "Your focus determines your reality!" When you dream, your mind forms a mental image, and the more you define it and think about it, the sharper and clearer your destiny becomes. Frame your dreams in long thoughts and circle them with hard prayers.

In 1992, Mark Tewksbury won the gold medal in the 200-meter backstroke at the Barcelona Olympics. When he stepped onto the platform to receive his medal, it wasn't his first time up there. He stood on the gold medal stand the night before the race and imagined it before it happened. He visualized every detail of the race in his mind's eye, including his come-from-behind victory by a fingertip.

The Australian sailing team did the same thing before the 1983 America's Cup. The coach made a tape (think pre-download, pre-CD) of the Australian team beating the American team three years before the race. He narrated the race with the background sound of a sailboat cutting through the water. Every teammate was required to listen to that tape twice a day for three years. By the time they set sail from San Diego Bay, they had already beaten the American team 2,190 times in their heads.

All this is what defines good goal setting. If dreams are the destination, goals are the GPS that gets you there. (Or the sailboat!)

Ten Steps to Goal Setting

"Ten Steps to Goal Setting" seems like the kind of book you pick up off your parents bookshelf, but you're getting this at the perfect time because you have your entire life in front of you. Before I share my life goal list, let me remind you that your goals are as unique as you are. They should reflect your unique personality and passions. But let these ten steps guide you in putting together your list.

1. Start with Prayer

Prayer is the best way to jump-start the process of goal setting. I highly recommend a personal retreat or season of fasting — whether it's stepping away from your cell phone for a week to focus on your goals, or planning to spend a block of time in a place you can think. I came up with my original life goal list during a two-day retreat at Rocky Gap Lodge in Cumberland, Maryland. The relaxed schedule gave me the time and space I needed to dream big, pray hard, and think long. My original list only contained twenty-five goals. During a ten-day fast a few years later I revised and expanded the list.

If you set goals in the context of prayer, there is a much higher likelihood that your goals will glorify God, and if they don't glorify God, then they aren't worth setting in the first place. Pray it out.

2. Check Your Motives

If you set selfish goals, you would be better off spiritually if you didn't accomplish them. That's why you need to check your motives. You need to take a long, honest look in the mirror and make sure you're going after your goals for the right reasons.

Prioritizing is important in checking motivation. "Travel goals" shouldn't outweigh "giving goals," for example. My motivation for making more money is giving more money. After all, you make a living by what you get, but you make a life by what you give.

3. Think in Categories

It is hard to pull life goals out of thin air, so I recommend looking at the life goal lists of others. But don't plagiarize!

Another trick that has helped me is thinking in categories. My goals are divided into five categories: (1) family, (2) influential, (3) experiential, (4) physical, and (5) travel.

You probably noticed a lack of the "Spiritual Goals" category, but that's because I try to put a spiritual spin on all my goals. Some of them are obviously spiritual, like taking each of my children on a mission trip or reading the Bible from cover to cover in seven different translations. But for me, running a triathlon with Parker was a spiritual experience! Goals that require physical discipline carry right over to spiritual disciple. Moral of the story: categorize your goals and try to put a spiritual attachment to them as best as possible.

4. Be Specific

Vague goals are lame goals! Same with prayer. If a goal isn't measurable, we have no way of knowing whether we've accomplished it. "Get better grades" is pretty weak. How do you know if you've accomplished it? Instead, target a specific GPA.

A great way to be specific is to attach ages to your goals. I want to run a triathlon in my forties, fifties, and sixties. Those are three separate goals that are time-stamped. One way to think long is to simply think ahead. What do you want to accomplish in ten or twenty or fifty years?

It wasn't easy to attach numbers to some of my giving and writing goals, but I decided it was better to aim high and fall short than to aim low and hit the target. And it's okay to modify your goals a little over the years too.

I can't exactly control how many books I sell, and that's never been my focus. I write because I'm called to write. But I was inspired by a goal that was set by Jack Canfield and Mark Hansen. They're coauthors of the Chicken Soup for the Soul series — the one you see *everywhere*. Their books have sold more than 80 million copies, and their 2020 goal is to sell a billion books and give $500 million to charity. I love the motivation and specificity of that goal!

One of the life goals that Lora and I have is to eventually live 90/10. In other words, we want to live off of 10 percent of our income and give away 90 percent. That goal was inspired by the one and only J.C. Penney, founder of the department store by the same name. He started out giving 10 percent and living off of 90 percent, but by the end of his life he was giving 90 percent and living off of 10 percent. Each year, Lora and I try to increase the percentage of income we're giving back to God. Living 80/20 and 50/50 are mile-markers along the way. Eventually, our goal is to reverse tithe: give God a 90/10 split.

Speaking of J.C. Penney, it's worth sharing what he said about the importance of goals. "Give me a stock clerk with a goal, and I will give you a man who will make history," said Penney. "Give me a man without a goal, and I will give you a stock clerk."

5. Write 'Em Down

One of my mottos is this: "The shortest pencil is longer than the longest memory." If you haven't written down your goals, you haven't really set them. Something powerful happens when you verbalize a goal, whether in a conversation or in a journal.

"Record the vision and inscribe it on tablets." [3] You know who said that? God did. On more than one occasion, I've been able to achieve a goal almost immediately after setting it. Just from simply putting my goals out there, I've had extremely generous people help me check off a few of my goals. In fact, several of them have been readers of this book. (No pressure, though!)

At some point in the process of goal setting, you need to muster the courage to verbalize it. That act of verbalization is an act of faith. When you write down a goal, it holds you accountable. The same goes for a prayer journal. A written prayer requires more faith simply because it's harder to write it than to say it. But the beautiful thing about written prayers, and prayer journals in particular, is that you have a written record of your prayer. That's why writing goals is important: you have a physical list to check off and tweak.

6. Include Others

I used to have a lot of personal goals, but I've recently replaced most of them with shared goals. Nothing cements a relationship like a shared goal! Goals are relationship glue. When you go after a goal with another person, it doubles the joy. Setting goals with a friend or family member is a way of seeking God together and having fun on the way.

One of my travel goals is to spend a night on Catalina Island with Lora. I fell in love with the idyllic island when I first visited it ten years ago. I strolled the streets and toured the town. I even checked off another life goal from my list by parasailing over the Pacific. It was a magical day, but I was by myself, and it wasn't the same without Lora. All day I kept thinking to myself, *I wish Lora was here.* So one of my goals is to take Lora there someday so we can experience it together.

If you have common interests, make a goal out of it. For example: Josiah is the biggest football fan in our family, so he got in on the goal of going to Super Bowl XLV with me. My daughter, Summer, is a gifted swimmer, so I thought swimming the Escape from Alcatraz would be a great goal for us to go after. And Parker has my adventure gene, so he went with me to Peru last year to hike the Inca Trail to Machu Picchu.

If you and your friend love hiking, indie music, photography, or traveling, turn it into a goal. Short-term goals are great, but also remember to think long. It can extend the life of a relationship as well!

7. Celebrate along the Way

When you accomplish a goal, celebrate it. When God answers a prayer, throw a party. We should celebrate as hard as we pray! One of my favorite Hebrew words is *ebenezer*. It means, "thus far the LORD has helped us."[4] When you accomplish a God-ordained goal, it's an *ebenezer* moment. You need to find a unique way to celebrate it and commemorate it. Whenever I write a new book, for example, our family celebrates with a special meal on the day the book is released. And I get to choose the restaurant!

I love traditions. One of my favorites is dinner at Tony Cheng's in Chinatown on New Year's Eve. We'll go around the table, sharing our favorite memories from the past year, and it's amazing how many of those memories were once goals. Taking Summer to her first Broadway play, learning to snowboard with Parker, and celebrating an anniversary in Italy with Lora are some of my greatest memories, but like all memories, they started out as goals. Setting goals is the way you turn imaginations into memories, and once you do, you need to celebrate them.

8. Dream Big

Your life goal list will include goals that are big and small. It'll include goals that are short-term and long-term. But I have one piece of advice: Make sure you have a few BHAGs on the list. You need some God-sized goals that qualify as crazy. Here's why: big goals turn us into big people.

One of my crazy goals is to make a movie. I have no idea how that's going to happen. It's a little more likely that I'll write a screenplay than land a role as a stunt double. But who knows? I have no idea how it'll happen, but this motivation traces all the way back to one of my earliest memories. I watched *The Hiding Place* when I was five and I put my faith in Christ. God used a movie to move me. I'd like to make a movie that does the same for someone else.

9. Think Long

Most of us overestimate what we can accomplish in two years, but we underestimate what we can accomplish in ten years. Remember that. If you want to dream big, you need to think long. Big dreams often translate into long goals. My goal of leading NCC to give $25 million to missions isn't going to happen next year! But we'll give faithfully and sacrificially, and over the next twenty-five years, we'll get there. The long-term aspect of goals is going to be hard because it's hard to think about the distant future when you're a teenager, but you've got to push yourself to make decisions now that will serve you well in ten or twenty years.

Is it possible for a man to dream continuously for seventy years? It was Honi's life question. If you want to dream until the day you die, you need to set goals that take a lifetime to achieve. And it's never too late to start! My uncle, Ken Knappen, always dreamed of writing a book, but he didn't accomplish that goal until he was in his eighties. *Is it possible for a man to dream continuously for seventy years?* Apparently it's possible to dream into your mid-eighties and beyond!

The sad truth is that most people spend more time planning their summer vacation than they do planning the rest of their life. That's poor stewardship of right-brain imagination. Goal setting is just good stewardship. Instead of just letting things happen to you, the goals you lay down will help you shape your own destiny. Instead of living out of memory, goals help you live out of imagination. Goals let you thrive, not just survive.

10. Pray Hard

Goal setting begins and ends with prayer. God-ordained goals are born from prayer, and prayer is what brings them to life. You need to keep circling your goals in prayer, like the Israelites circled Jericho. As you circle your goals, it not only creates God-ordained opportunities; it also helps you recognize God-ordained opportunities by sanctifying your reticular activating system.

The Reticular Activating System

The reticular activating system is a group of nerve cells located at the base of the brain. We're constantly bombarded by countless things competing for our attention, and it's the reticular activating system's job to determine what gets noticed and what gets ignored. It determines what is important enough for your personal attention.

When God gave us the dream of starting a coffeehouse, I immediately started noticing all the details of every coffeehouse I visited. Before the dream, the only thing I noticed was the taste of my drink. After the dream, I noticed everything from signage and seating to store layout and product branding. The dream of starting a coffee-house created a category in my reticular activating system, and I started collecting ideas.

This is why goal setting is so important. It creates a category in your reticular activating system, and you start noticing anything and everything that will help you accomplish the goal. Prayer is important for the same reason. It sanctifies your RAS so you notice what God wants you to notice. The more you pray, the more you notice.

Paul, in his letter to the Colossians, said: "Devote yourselves to prayer, being watchful and thankful."[5] The word *watchful* is a throw-back to the ancient watchmen whose job it was to sit on the city walls and scan the horizon for attacking armies or trading caravans. They saw sooner and further than anyone else. Prayer opens our spiritual eyes so we see sooner and further.

The Aramaic word for *prayer*, in this instance, literally means "to set a trap." Prayer is the way we take thoughts and dreams and ideas captive. And one way to set prayer traps is by keeping a prayer journal. In my opinion, journaling is one of the most overlooked and under-appreciated spiritual disciplines. Journaling is the difference between learning and remembering. It's also the difference between forgetting and fulfilling our goals.

Life Goal List

If you want to see my life goal list, I've included it in the appendix of the book. I thought it would be even better if you got to see Parker's goal list. We actually share quite a few goals in common. It's double the fun going after those goals together! The goals that are italicized are the ones that have already been accomplished at the time of this writing.

Goals for my Kin:
- ☐ 1. Marry a girl. Stay married for 50 years.
- ☐ 2. Have a son. Name him Ronin.
- ☐ 3. Take all of my kids to every continent minus Antarctica.
- ☐ 4. Take all of my kids on a pilgrimage to the Holy Land.

☐ 5. Pay for a grandchild to go to college.

☑ 6. *Go to Third World country with my brother.*

☐ 7. Take all my kids camping around the world.

☐ 8. Carry on Discipleship Covenant tradition with my kids.

☐ 9. Sail around the Cape of Good Hope with my wife.

☐ 10. Visit a film festival with my brother.

☐ 11. Take my sister to a fashion show in Milan.

Goals for my Impact:

☐ 12. Write 10 books.

☐ 13. Speak at a TED conference.

☐ 14. Present a movie I made at a film festival.

☐ 15. Write an autobiography.

☐ 16. Publish a scientific journal.

☐ 17. Go on an archaeological dig.

☐ 18. Own a company/business.

☐ 19. Have a piece of my art put into an art museum (someone might need to check this off for me after I die).

☐ 20. Write a book that someone influential reads.

Experience Goals:

☐ 21. Learn Arabic.

☑ 22. *Learn Latin.*

☐ 23. Run with the Bulls in Pamplona, Spain.

☐ 24. Visit all 50 states.

☑ 25. *Learn to sail.*

☐ 26. Visit all 7 continents.

☐ 27. Learn to fly.

☑ 28. *Learn to fence the Epee.*

☑ 29. *Play Rugby.*

☐ 30. Go Big Game hunting.

☑ 31. *Go cliff jumping.*

☐ 32. Go skydiving.

☑ 33. *Go paragliding.*

☐ 34. Spend a month surviving in Alaska.

☑ 35. *Go horseback riding.*

☐ 36. Scuba dive the Great Barrier Reef.

☑ 37. *See Old Faithful in Yellow Stone.*

☐ 38. Experience a mass baptism.

Goals for my Body:

☑ 39. *Bike a century.*

☐ 40. Run a marathon.

☑ 41. *Run a triathlon.*

☐ 42. Run an Olympic-distance triathlon.

☑ 43. *Learn to snowboard.*

☐ 44. Learn to surf.

☐ 45. Take a vow of silence for a week.

☐ 46. Fast from all food for 5 days.

☐ 47. Climb Mt. Kilimanjaro.

☐ 48. Climb K2.

☐ 49. Climb El Capitan in 3 days.

☑ 50. *Hike the Inca Trail in Peru.*

☑ 51. *Hike the Grand Canyon from rim to rim.*

☐ 52. See Switchfoot in concert 5 times.

☐ 53. Visit the Castle Church in Wittenberg, Germany.

☐ 54. Break a world record.

☐ 55. Memorize a book of the Bible.

☐ 56. Watch a volcano erupt.

Goals for my Finances:

☐ 57. Own a house.

☐ 58. Own an art studio.

☐ 59. Retire by fifty.

☐ 60. Give someone random in need $100,000.

☐ 61. Live 90/10 by the time I die.

Miscellaneous Goals:

- ☐ 62. Meet a president.
- ☐ 63. Meet Bear Grylls.
- ☑ 64. *Meet Jeff Corwin.*
- ☐ 65. Save someone's life.
- ☐ 66. Kiss my future wife on Rialto Bridge in Venice.
- ☑ 67. *Straddle the Equator.*
- ☐ 68. See the aurora borealis.
- ☐ 69. Go boar hunting with a spear.
- ☑ 70. *See a rodeo.*
- ☐ 71. Be baptized in the Jordan River.
- ☐ 72. Fill a sketchbook with 100 good drawings.
- ☐ 73. Create a 15-foot-tall sculpture.
- ☑ 74. *Make a video of a family vacation for my family.*
- ☐ 75. Buy a horse.
- ☐ 76. Make a sword.
- ☐ 77. Get sponsored by Red Bull to do something crazy.
- ☐ 78. Build a log cabin.
- ☐ 79. Ride an elephant.

Draw the Circle

1. Have you ever made a list of life goals? If you have, take time to review and revise. If you have not, spend some time praying and goal-setting.

2. Are there any dreams or goals that have gone unaccomplished because you haven't given yourself a deadline? If so, give yourself a deadline now. Take some first steps. And ask a friend to hold you accountable.

3. Which life goals from the book are on your list as well? Are there any in these lists that have given you ideas?

Part 4

Keep Circling

The most recent life goal checked off my list was hiking Half Dome in Yosemite National Park with Parker. (If you looked at my goals in the Appendix, you'll probably notice it was on the list.) In terms of degree of difficulty, it ranks right behind hiking the Inca Trail to Machu Picchu and hiking the Grand Canyon from rim to rim. It was a 15.5-mile hike with a 4,800-foot ascent. But the hardest part wasn't the physical challenge; the hardest part was facing my fear of heights and climbing the cables that scaled the sixty-degree slope to the summit.

On the morning of the hike, I glanced up at Half Dome from the valley floor, and I just thought, *How in the world are we supposed to get up there?* It seemed next to impossible, but the answer was quite simple: *one step at a time.* That's how you accomplish any goal. You can climb the highest mountain if you put one foot in front of the other and refuse to stop until you reach the top. It took a lot of drive, and I was running on reserves by the end, but you have to remember that each step is progress. Glance up to the ultimate goal often, but keep focused on every step forward.

Drawing prayer circles is a lot like climbing a mountain. With each prayer, there is a small change in elevation. With each prayer, you're at least one step closer to the answer.

After conquering Half Dome, I came to this realization: The degree of satisfaction is absolutely relative to the degree of difficulty. The harder the climb, the sweeter the summit. The same is true with prayer. The more you have to circle something in prayer, the more satisfying it is spiritually. And, often, the more glory God gets.

Until recently, I wanted God to answer every prayer ASAP. That is no longer my agenda. I don't even *want* easy or quick answers because I have a tendency to mishandle the blessings that come too easily or too quickly. I take the credit or take them for granted. So now I pray that it'll take long enough and be hard enough for God to receive full glory. I'm not looking for the path of least resistance; I'm looking for the path of greatest glory. And that requires high-degree-of-difficulty prayers and lots of circling!

Very rarely does our first prayer request hit the bull's-eye of God's good, pleasing, and perfect will. You're never going to get it right the first time, every time. Most prayer requests have to be refined. Even "the prayer that saved a generation" didn't hit the bull's-eye the first time. Honi refined his request twice: "Not for such rain have I prayed." He wasn't satisfied with a sprinkle or torrential downpour. It took three attempts to spell out exactly what he wanted: "rain of Your favor, blessing, *and* graciousness." Honi drew a circle in the sand. Then he drew a circle within a circle within a circle.

One of the reasons we get frustrated in prayer is our ASAP approach. When our prayers aren't answered as quickly or easily as we would like, we get tired of circling. Maybe we need to change our prayer approach from *as soon as possible* to *as long as it takes*.

Keep circling!

Chapter 16

Now There Was One

Josephus was a famous Jewish historian. In his epic history *Antiquities of the Jews*, he notes the deeds of Honi the circle maker, aka Onias the rainmaker. He documents the first-century drought and points to Honi as Israel's only hope. Josephus makes one little statement that I think is important: "now there was one."

> Now there was one, whose name was Onias, a righteous man he was, and beloved of God, who, in a certain drought, prayed to God to put an end to the intense heat, and whose prayers God had heard, and had sent them rain.[1]

Honi stood alone. Then he knelt down in the circle he had drawn. And that's all it takes to change the course of His-story. In the words of theologian Walter Wink, "History belongs to the intercessors."[2]

After the rain fell and the dust settled, Simeon ben Shatah, the ruling head of the Sanhedrin who threatened excommunication from the synagogue, wrote to Honi:

> Were you not Honi, I should decree excommunication against you ... But what can I do to you, for you act petulantly before the Omnipresent and he does whatever you want for you ...
>
> A generation that was shrouded in darkness did you illuminate through your prayer ... A generation that was sunk down you lifted up with your prayer ... A generation that was humiliated by its sin you saved by your prayer.[3]

Never underestimate the power of one prayer circle.

When you dream big, pray hard, and think long, there's nothing

God can't use you for. After all, He's able to do 15.5 billion light-years *more* than what you can ask or imagine. When you draw a circle and drop to your knees, *you can't never always sometimes tell*. It changes the forecast of your life. It's always cloudy with a chance of quail.

You can't always fell a fifty-foot wall, but you can march around it. You can't shut the mouths of lions, but you can stop, drop, and pray. You can't make it rain, but you can draw a circle in the sand.

Don't let what you cannot do keep you from doing what you can. Draw the circle. Don't let who you aren't keep you from being who you are. You're a circle maker.

One Prayer Circle

Rodney "Gypsy" Smith was born in a gypsy camp on the outskirts of London in 1860. He never got a formal education, yet he was asked to lecture at Harvard. Despite his humble origins, two sitting presidents invited him to the White House. Gypsy crisscrossed the Atlantic Ocean forty-five times, preaching the gospel to millions of people. Few people have been more powerfully used by God. Everywhere he went, it seemed like revival was right on his heels. But it wasn't his preaching that brought revival. It never is. Preaching may move the hearts of men, but praying moves the heart of God. And that's where revival always starts.

One day a delegation of revival-seekers sought an audience with Gypsy. They wanted to know how they could make a difference with their lives the way he had with his. His answer was simple yet profound. And it's as timely and timeless now as it was a hundred years ago. He gave them this advice:

> Go home. Lock yourself in your bedroom. Take a piece of chalk and draw a circle on your bedroom floor. Then kneel in that circle and pray fervently and brokenly that God would start a revival in that circle.

Now there was one.
All it takes is one person. One prayer.
Why not you?

It's as simple as drawing your first prayer circle, just like I did when I prayed all the way around Capitol Hill. It might be a promise or a problem. It might be a friend or an enemy. It might be a dream or a miracle. I don't know how it's spelled, but it's your job to spell it out. Then keep circling.

I wouldn't recommend doing this by yourself. Israel had an army! Invite others into your prayer circle. Together you'll form a prayer circle, and when two or three agree in prayer, double circling their God-sized and God-ordained goals, all bets are off.

Echo through Eternity

At the end of our prayers, we say "Amen," which means, "so be it." It signifies the end of a prayer. But the end of a prayer is always just the beginning. It's the beginning of a dream. It's the beginning of a miracle. It's the beginning of a promise. Remember that prayers are like living things. When the prayer comes out of you, it's just being born and has an endless lifetime to be fulfilled!

The legend of Honi the circle maker began with a prayer for rain. Now it's time to reveal the *amen*.

In 63 BC, Palestine was torn in two by a bloody civil war. Hyrcanus II and Aristobulus II (both sons of Alexander Jannaeus, king of Judea) met in battle near Jericho. Aristobulus was forced to flee to the temple in Jerusalem to make his last stand. Hyrcanus and his ally, the Arabian sheik Aretas, surrounded the temple with fifty thousand troops. The priests and temple guards were the only ones to stand by Aristobulus.

That's when the army of Hyrcanus found the old rainmaker, Honi, who had been in hiding. The superstitious army brought Honi to Hyrcanus, who commanded the prophet to put a curse on the defenders of the temple. Honi didn't obey his command, even with a sword at his throat! Like the prophet Balaam, who refused to curse Israel and prayed a blessing according to his conscience, Honi drew his last circle in the sand.

In one of history's sad ironies, the man who saved a generation with his prayer for rain was put to death because of a prayer that went against the wishes of Hyrcanus. But Honi stayed true to his convictions, not just in life, but also in death. Many years before, a crowd of thirsty souls surrounded Honi as he drew his circle in the sand. Now he was surrounded by thugs whose lives he had saved with his prayer for rain. They forced him to speak, so Honi uttered his last words while living on this earth, but it's a prayer that'll echo through all eternity.

> O God, the King of the whole world! since those that stand now with me are Your people, and those that are besieged are also Your priests, I beseech You that You will neither hearken to the prayers of those against these, nor bring to effect what these pray against those.[4]

That's when the mob turned on Honi and stoned the circle maker to death. It may seem like a tragic ending, but Honi died the way he lived. He prayed until the day he died. His dying breath was a prayer that carried him into eternity. I don't think the circle maker would have had it any other way.

What a way to live.

What a way to die.

What a way to enter eternity!

Draw the Circle

1. Walter Wink said, "History belongs to the intercessors." What did he mean by this? Why is this so important to understand and believe?

2. Which of your friends do you need to invite into your prayer circle? What dream, problem, or challenge will you circle in prayer together?

3. Make your own prayer circle. Get down on your knees. Seek God for personal revival in your life.

Appendix

In case you were wondering, I've included my own life goal list here:

Mark's Life Goal List

Family Goals

- [ ] 1. Celebrate our fiftieth wedding anniversary.
- [ ] 2. Dedicate my great-grandchildren to the Lord.
- [x] 3. *Celebrate an anniversary in Italy.*
- [ ] 4. Celebrate an anniversary in the Caribbean.
- [ ] 5. Take each child on a mission trip.
- [x] 6. *Coach a sports team for each child.*
- [ ] 7. Pay for our grandchildren's college education.
- [x] 8. *Create a family foundation.*
- [ ] 9. Leave an inheritance for our children.
- [ ] 10. Write an autobiography.
- [x] 11. *Create a discipleship covenant.*
- [ ] 12. Take each child on a rite of passage pilgrimage.
- [x] 13. *Create a family coat of arms.*
- [ ] 14. Research our family genealogy.
- [ ] 15. Find and visit an ancestor's grave in Sweden.
- [ ] 16. Take our grandchildren to a state fair.
- [ ] 17. Go on a camping trip with our grandchildren.
- [ ] 18. Take our grandchildren to Disney World.
- [ ] 19. Celebrate a family reunion on a cruise ship.
- [ ] 20. Celebrate a family reunion in Alexandria, Minnesota.

Influence Goals

- [ ] 21. Write twenty-five-plus nonfiction books.
- [ ] 22. Pastor one church for forty-plus years.

☐ 23. Help 1,000,000 dads disciple their sons.

☐ 24. Speak at a college commencement.

☑ 25. *Speak at an NFL chapel.*

☐ 26. Write a *New York Times* bestseller.

☐ 27. Write a fiction title.

☑ 28. *Start a mentoring group for pastors.*

☐ 29. Create a conference for writers.

☑ 30. *Create a conference for pastors.*

☑ 31. *Teach a college course.*

☐ 32. Lead National Community Church to 10,000-plus in weekly attendance.

☐ 33. Baptize 3,000 people in the same place at the same time.

☐ 34. Build an orphanage in Ethiopia.

☐ 35. Build a vacation home.

☐ 36. Get a doctoral degree.

☐ 37. Start a chain of coffeehouses that give their net profits to kingdom causes.

☐ 38. Help plant 100-plus churches.

☐ 39. Make a movie.

☐ 40. Host a radio or television program.

Experiential Goals

☑ 41. *Take Summer to a Broadway play.*

☑ 42. *Hike the Inca Trail to Machu Picchu with Parker.*

☑ 43. *Go to a Super Bowl with Josiah.*

☐ 44. Spend a night on Catalina Island with Lora.

☑ 45. *Go paragliding with Parker.*

☐ 46. Go skydiving.

☐ 47. Go cliff jumping.

☐ 48. Go to a cowboy camp with my boys.

☐ 49. Take Parker to a film festival.

☑ 50. *Learn how to snowboard.*

☐ 51. Learn how to surf.

☑ 52. *Take a helicopter ride over the Grand Canyon.*

☐ 53. Take a rafting trip through the Grand Canyon.

☐ 54. Take a three-month sabbatical.

☐ 55. Do a silent retreat at a monastery.

☐ 56. Go on an overnight canoe trip with one of my kids.

☐ 57. Drive a race car with one of my kids.

☐ 58. Read the Bible from cover to cover in seven translations.

☐ 59. Take a hot air balloon ride.

☑ 60. *Go horseback riding as a family.*

☐ 61. Spend a night in a tree house hotel.

☑ 62. *Go to a Packers' game at Lambeau Field.*

☐ 63. Hike the Camino de Santiago in Spain.

☐ 64. Run with the bulls in Pamplona.

☑ 65. *Play a round of golf at St. Andrews in Scotland.*

☑ 66. *See the Stone of Destiny at Edinburgh Castle.*

☐ 67. Do a stand-up comedy routine.

☐ 68. Take Lora to the Oscars.

☐ 69. Go to a TED Conference.

☐ 70. Take a mission trip to five different continents.

Physical Goals

☑ 71. *Hike the Grand Canyon from rim to rim.*

☐ 72. Climb a 14er (mountain over 14,000 feet tall).

☐ 73. Swim the Escape from Alcatraz with Summer.

☐ 74. Run a 10K with one of our kids.

☐ 75. Run a triathlon with Parker and Josiah.

☐ 76. Dunk a basketball in my forties.

☐ 77. Bench-press 250-plus pounds in my fifties.

☐ 78. Run a triathlon in my sixties.

☑ 79. *Run a half marathon.*

☐ 80. Bike a century (100-mile trip).

☐ 81. Run an urbanathlon (urban obstacle-course race).

Financial Goals

- ☐ 82. Be debt free by fifty-five.
- ☐ 83. Give back every penny we've earned from National Community Church.
- ☐ 84. Live off 10 percent and give 90 percent by the time we retire.
- ☐ 85. Give away $10-plus million.
- ☐ 86. Lead National Community Church to give $25,000,000 to missions.

Travel Goals

- ☐ 87. Retrace one of Paul's missionary journeys.
- ☐ 88. Take an RV vacation as a family.
- ☑ 89. *Hike to the top of Half Dome in Yosemite National Park.*
- ☑ 90. *Stay at the Ahwahnee Hotel in Yosemite.*
- ☑ 91. *Visit the Biltmore mansion.*
- ☑ 92. *Stay at Old Faithful Inn in Yellowstone National Park.*
- ☑ 93. *Hike to Inspiration Point near Jenny Lake in Grand Teton National Park.*
- ☑ 94. *Go to a Western rodeo.*
- ☐ 95. Climb to the rock-hewn churches in Lalibela, Ethiopia.
- ☐ 96. Visit the monasteries of Meteora in Greece.
- ☐ 97. Go on an African safari.
- ☐ 98. Walk the Via Dolorosa in the Holy Land.
- ☐ 99. Visit Jerusalem during a Jewish holiday.
- ☐ 100. See a kangaroo in Australia.
- ☐ 101. Snorkel the Great Barrier Reef in Australia.
- ☐ 102. Kiss Lora on top of the Eiffel Tower in France.
- ☐ 103. Climb Mount Kilimanjaro.
- ☐ 104. See the aurora borealis.
- ☐ 105. Go kayaking in Alaska.
- ☑ 106. *Visit the Castle Church in Wittenberg, Germany.*
- ☐ 107. Take a boat cruise down the Rhine River.
- ☐ 108. Ride a gondola in Venice.

☐ 109. See the sunrise on Cadillac Mountain in Acadia National Park.

☐ 110. Hike the trails in Haleakala National Park in Hawaii.

☑ 111. *Straddle the equator.*

☑ 112. *See the Blue Grotto sea cave in Italy.*

☐ 113. Visit the Parthenon in Athens, Greece.

☐ 114. Take a carriage ride through Central Park in New York City.

☐ 115. Stay at the Grand Hotel on Mackinac Island.

Notes

Chapter 1: The Legend of the Circle Maker

1. Page 9: *His name was Honi*: To read more about Honi, see "The Deeds of the Sages," in *The Book of Legends: Sefer Ha-Aggadah*, ed. Hayim Nahman Bialik and Yehoshua Hana Ravnitzky (New York: Schocken, 1992), 202–3. See also Abraham Cohen, *Everyman's Talmud* (New York: Schocken, 1995), 277, and Henry Malter, *The Treatise Ta'anit of the Babylonian Talmud* (Philadelphia: Jewish Publication Society, 1978), 270. Note: Honi the circle maker is sometimes referred to as Choni the circle maker, Honi Ha-Me'aggel, and Onias the rainmaker.

Chapter 2: Circle Makers

1. Page 13: *God is for you*: Romans 8:31.
2. Page 15: *"I'm giving you every square inch"*: Joshua 1:3 MSG.
3. Page 15: *I had a Honi-like confidence*: Notice that the promise was originally given to Moses. The promise was then transferred to Joshua. In much the same way, all of God's promises have been transferred to us via Jesus Christ. While promises must be interpreted and applied in an accurate historical and exegetical fashion, there are moments when the Spirit of God quickens our spirit and transfers a promise that He had originally given to someone else. While we have to be careful not to blindly claim promises, I think our greatest challenge is that we don't circle as many promises as we could or should.

Chapter 3: The Jericho Miracle

1. Page 19: *They finally understood why*: Numbers 13:33.
2. Page 20: *Your entire army is to march*: See Joshua 6:3–4.
3. Page 21: *"What do you want me to do for you?"*: Matthew 20:31–32.
4. Page 24: *Then we wrote down our holy desires*: According to Psalm 37:4, God actually downloads new desires in our hearts when we genuinely seek His glory. Those desires are often conceived in the context of prayer and fasting. It takes tremendous discernment to distinguish between holy desires and selfish desires.
5. Page 28: *If you think of a problem*: Quoted in M. Mitchell Waldrop, *Complexity: The Emerging Science at the Edge of Order and Chaos* (New York: Simon & Schuster, 1992), 29.

Chapter 4: Praying Through

1. Page 32: *Lord, if you will bless my husband*: Mother Elizabeth J. Dabney, "Praying Through," www.charismamag.com/index.php/newsletters/spiritled-woman-emagazine/22087-forerunners-of-faith-praying-through (accessed June 7, 2011).

2. Page 33: *Like the story Jesus told*: Luke 18:1–8.

3. Page 37: *"gates of Jericho were securely barred"*: Joshua 6:1–2.

Part 1: The First Circle—Dream Big

1. Page 39: *Is it possible for a man to dream*: Henry Malter, *The Treatise Ta'anit of the Babylonian Talmud* (Philadelphia: Jewish Publication Society, 1978), 270.

Chapter 5: Cloudy with a Chance of Quail

1. Page 44: *"The people of Israel also began to complain"*: Numbers 11:4–6 NLT.

2. Page 45: *"Here I am among six hundred thousand men"*: Numbers 11:21–22.

3. Page 47: *"How far will they go among so many?"*: John 6:9.

4. Page 48: *"So Moses went out and told the people"*: Numbers 11:24.

5. Page 50: *"Now a wind went out from the LORD"*: Numbers 11:31–32.

Chapter 6: You Can't Never Always Sometimes Tell

1. Page 58: *"One day at about three"*: Acts 10:3.

2. Page 59: *"prayed to God regularly"*: Acts 10:2.

3. Page 59: *"amazed and perplexed"*: Acts 2:12.

4. Page 60: *"Surely not, Lord!"*: Acts 10:14.

5. Page 60: Scripture says he was *"very perplexed"*: Acts 10:17 NLT.

6. Page 60: *"I have never eaten anything impure"*: Acts 10:14.

Chapter 7: The Solution to Ten Thousand Problems

1. Page 65: *"Is there a limit to my power?"*: Numbers 11:23 GNT.

2. Page 68: *"Is the LORD's arm too short?"*: Numbers 11:23 NIV; *"Is the LORD's hand waxed short?"*: Numbers 11:23 KJV.

3. Page 68: *"This is the finger of God"*: Exodus 8:19.

4. Page 69: *"As the heavens are higher than the earth"*: Isaiah 55:9.

Part 2: The Second Circle—Pray Hard

1. Page 75: *"One day Jesus told his disciples a story"*: Luke 18:1–5 NLT.

Chapter 8: Persistence Quotient

1. Page 79: *The American children lasted, on average, 9.47 minutes*: Malcolm Gladwell, *Outliers* (New York: Little, Brown, 2008), 249.

2. Page 80: *the average players had logged*: Gladwell, *Outliers*, 38–39.

3. Page 80: *"The emerging picture from such studies"*: Daniel Levitin, *This Is Your Brain on Music: The Science of a Human Obsession* (New York: Penguin, 2007), 193.

4. Page 81: *it wasn't a light drizzle*: 1 Kings 18:45.

5. Page 82: *"Lord, if you had been here"*: John 11:21–22.

6. Page 84: *"No matter how many promises"*: 2 Corinthians 1:20.

Chapter 9: The Favor of Him Who Dwells in the Burning Bush

1. Page 90: *has been voted the #1 coffeehouse*: Washington, DC, metro area, *AOL City Guide, 2008.*
2. Page 91: *Elijah won that sudden-death showdown*: 1 Kings 18:38.
3. Page 91: *"whatever you bind on earth"*: Matthew 18:18.
4. Page 92: *The Lord is watching over His word*: Jeremiah 1:12 ESV.
5. Page 92: *He is actively watching and waiting*: Matthew 8:8 is a great example of this kind of faith. The Roman centurion doesn't ask Jesus to come and heal his child. He simply says, "Just say the word." He had an inherent belief that God's word was His bond. And it says that Jesus "was amazed." If you amaze the Son of God, you've done something significant.
6. Page 92: *"No good thing does [God] withhold"*: Psalm 84:11 ESV.
7. Page 93: *"Surely goodness and mercy shall follow me"*: Psalm 23:6 ESV.
8. Page 94: *"Now is the time of God's favor"*: 2 Corinthians 6:2.
9. Page 94: *"May the LORD bless his land"*: Deuteronomy 33:13–16.
10. Page 96: *"Let my people go"*: Exodus 5:1.

Chapter 10: Game of Chicken

1. Page 100: *He did it with the widow*: 2 Kings 4:1–7.
2. Page 100: *He did it when the Israelites are trapped*: Exodus 14:21–31.
3. Page 100: *He did it when the boat is about to capsize*: Matthew 8:23–27.
4. Page 100: *When God provided the miraculous manna*: Exodus 16:4.
5. Page 100: *"Do not keep any of it until morning"*: Exodus 16:19 NLT.
6. Page 100: *"Give us today our daily bread"*: Matthew 6:11.
7. Page 104: *"When you reach the banks"*: Joshua 3:8 NLT.
8. Page 105: *"Come"*: Matthew 14:29.
9. Page 106: *"After Jesus and his disciples arrived"*: Matthew 17:24–27.

Chapter 11: No Answer

1. Page 112: *"What have I done to you"*: Numbers 22:28.
2. Page 113: *"I have come here to oppose you"*: Numbers 22:32–33.
3. Page 117: *"Do not be afraid. Stand firm"*: Exodus 14:13–14.

Part 3: The Third Circle—Think Long

1. Page 123: *After a little historical research, it was discovered*: Stewart Brand, *The Clock of the Long Now: Time and Responsibility* (New York: Basic, 1999), 162.

Chapter 12: Long and Boring

1. Page 126: *"Now when Daniel learned"*: Daniel 6:10.

2. Page 127: *Daniel prophesied that it would take*: Daniel 9:2.

Chapter 13: The Greatest of Them All

1. Page 136: *"Go and pray, Connie"*: Conrad Hilton, *Be My Guest* (New York: Simon and Schuster, 1994), 17.

2. Page 136: *"In the circle of successful living"*: Hilton, *Be My Guest*, 288.

3. Page 138: "I will give you every place": Joshua 1:3.

4. Page 139: *New York University psychologist John Bargh*: Cited in Malcolm Gladwell, *Blink: The Power of Thinking without Thinking* (New York: Little, Brown and Company, 2005), 53–57.

5. Page 140: *"fearfully and wonderfully made"*: Psalm 139:14.

6. Page 141: *Dutch researchers did a similar priming experiment*: Gladwell, *Blink*, 56.

7. Page 141: *"In the morning, LORD"*: Psalm 5:3.

8. Page 143: *He loved to pray early in the morning*: Mark 1:35.

9. Page 144: *"I will stand upon my watch"*: Habakkuk 2:1, quoted in *The Book of Legends: Sefer Ha-Aggadah*, ed. Hayim Nahman Bialik and Yehoshua Hana Ravnitzky (New York: Schocken, 1992), 202.

10. Page 146: *"We try to call Him to mind"*: Frank Laubach, *The Game with Minutes* (Westwood, N.J.: Revell, 1961).

11. Page 147: *"Last Monday was the most completely successful"*: Brother Lawrence and Frank Laubach, *Practicing His Presence* (Goleta, Calif.: Christian Books, 1973), June 1, 1930 entry.

Chapter 14: The Speed of Prayer

1. Page 151: *"Do not be afraid, Daniel"*: Daniel 10:12–14.

2. Page 154: *"The moment you began praying"*: Daniel 9:23 NLT.

3. Page 155: *"Daniel resolved not to defile himself"*: Daniel 1:8.

4. Page 156: *"Couldn't you men keep watch"*: Matthew 26:40.

5. Page 156: *"The spirit is willing"*: Matthew 26:41.

6. Page 157: *"I am the vine, you are the branches"*: John 15:5 NASB.

Chapter 15: Life Goal List

1. Page 161: *In his groundbreaking book*: Jim Collins and Jerry Porras, *Built to Last* (New York: HarperCollins, 1994), 93.

2. Page 162: *Scripture says that without a vision*: Proverbs 29:18 KJV.

3. Page 165: *"Record the vision and inscribe it"*: Habakkuk 2:2 NASB.

4. Page 166: *"Thus far the LORD has helped us"*: 1 Samuel 7:12.

5. Page 169: *"Devote yourselves to prayer"*: Colossians 4:2.

Chapter 16: Now There Was One

1. Page 175: *"Now there was one"*: Flavius Josephus, *Jewish Antiquities* (London: Wordsworth, 2006), 581.

2. Page 175: *"History belongs to the intercessors"*: This is one of my all-time favorite sayings, but I want to share the larger context of the statement (from Walter Wink's *The Powers That Be: Theology for a New Millennium* [New York: Doubleday, 1999], 185–86).

Intercessory prayer is spiritual defiance of what is in the way of what God has promised. Intercession visualizes an alternative future to the one apparently fated by the momentum of current forces. Prayer infuses the air of a time yet to be into the suffocating atmosphere of the present.

History belongs to the intercessors who believe the future into being. This is not simply a religious statement. It is also true of Communists or capitalists or anarchists. The future belongs to whoever can envision a new and desirable possibility, which faith then fixes upon as inevitable.

This is the politics of hope. Hope envisages its future and then acts as if that future is now irresistible, thus helping to create the reality for which it longs. The future is not closed. There are fields of forces whose actions are somewhat predictable. But how they will interact is not. Even a small number of people, firmly committed to the new inevitability on which they have fixed their imaginations, can decisively affect the shape the future takes.

These shapers of the future are the intercessors, who call out of the future the longed-for new present. In the New Testament, the name and texture and aura of that future is God's domination-free order, the reign of God.

No doubt our intercessions sometimes change us as we open ourselves to new possibilities we had not guessed. No doubt our prayers to God reflect back upon us as a divine command to become the answer to our prayer. But if we are to take the biblical understanding seriously, intercession is more than that. It changes the world and it changes what is possible to God. It creates an island of relative freedom in a world gripped by unholy necessity. A new force field appears that hitherto was only potential. The entire configuration changes as the result of the change of a single part. A space opens in the praying person, permitting God to act without violating human freedom. The change in one person thus changes what God can thereby do in that world.

3. Page 175: *"Were you not Honi"*: Jacob Neusner, *The Talmud: Law, Knowledge, Narrative* (Lanham, Md.: University Press of America, 2005), 183.

4. Page 178: *"O God, the King of the whole world"*: Lawrence H. Schiffman, *Texts and Traditions: A Source Reader for the Study of Second Temple and Rabbinic Judaism* (Hoboken, N.J.: KTAV Publishing House, 1998), 261.

The Circle Maker Prayer Journal

Mark Batterson

One of the single-most power-ful ways to improve your prayer life and build your faith is to keep a prayer journal to record your prayers and God's an-swers. With its supple leather-like binding, *The Circle Maker Prayer Journal* includes inspirational quotes from Mark Batterson, author of the *New York Times* bestseller *The Circle Maker*, and is a powerful tool for your own amazing prayer journey.

Talk It Up!

Want free books?
First looks at the best new fiction?
Awesome exclusive merchandise?

We want to hear from you!

Give us your opinions on titles, covers, and stories.
Join the Z Street Team.

Visit zstreetteam.zondervan.com/joinnow
to sign up today!

Also—Friend us on Facebook!

www.facebook.com/goodteenreads

- Video Trailers

- Connect with your favorite authors

- Sneak peeks at new releases

- Giveaways

- Fun discussions

- And much more!

ZONDERVAN®
.com